How to begin a speech?

100 ideas for 1000 custom beginnings

Michael Rossié

Convincing right from the start

Impressum

Bibliografische Information der Deutschen Nationalbibliothek:
Die Deutsche Nationalbibliothek verzeichnet diese
Publikation in der Deutschen Nationalbibliografie;
detaillierte bibliografische Daten sind im Internet über
http://dnb.dnb.de abrufbar.

© 2022 Michael Rossié

Proofreading: Thomas Bächle
Cover photo: Astrid M. Obert

Herstellung und Verlag: BoD – Books on Demand,
Norderstedt

ISBN: 978-3-755766728

Content

> "In every beginning lives a magic hold"
> Hermann Hesse

Foreword

This book shows you 100 different possibilities on how to begin a speech in a very impressive way. In real life there are not exactly 100 ways to begin a speech neither have I found, in years of research, the 100 ultimate beginnings. The reason for the title is that the capacity of the book is limited.

Just as there are endless ways to begin a conversation or to address someone, there are endless ways to start a speech. Let yourself be inspired and take a few suggestions. Every example should help you to find an idea of your own, so that you are able to say: Great! I will begin my speech just like that. My wife discovered her favorite beginning immediately, when she was correcting this book.

Additionally, I will present to you the eleven beginnings that I would avoid or at least would improve. Many beginnings are superfluous and boring.

When you have finished reading this book and you are able to give a thrilling, unconventional and just different speech, then the aim of the book has been achieved. Because audiences don't love anything more than being stimulated, impressed or surprised. And they don't hate anything more than being bored. Therefore, it won't matter what you are talking about.

As soon as you stand in front of a group, you are stealing a large amount of people's time. Be careful with it! Then people will come and listen to you a second time.

Imagine the following: The group in front of you is a living creature, a creature that consists of many small organisms. And these organisms can get their own dynamic very quickly, which you won't be able to control any longer. Spectators are voluntarily quiet once they decide that you are allowed to present. However they can change their mind at any time. They can decide to heckle, to laugh sarcastically or stand up, leave the room and slam the door.

It is a very special moment when hundreds of people decide to be quiet from the beginning for a longer time and to listen to just one single person. This is an acknowledgment, this is an honor, and this is a little miracle. The thrill couldn't be greater.

Everything which follows now shows the direction, it defines the tone and it fulfills the expectations – or perhaps not. Now is the moment of truth whether it was valuable to dress up elegantly, to jump into the next traffic jam and to pay the expensive babysitter

Don't let this special opportunity go to waste, make it a great moment.

Have fun!

Michael

Introduction

Many, many years ago a film in cinema or on TV began with long opening credits, where fitting music was played when the cast was presented.

On the first twenty pages of a book, the acting characters were presented before they had their first adventure together. At school the teacher explained, that a speech requires an introduction at the beginning.

In this book there are no tips for introductions, but for beginnings. It doesn't matter whether it is a speech, a video clip, a podcast or a televised interview

Today we begin directly: we start, we fight for attention, we want attentiveness. When we get it, it is still possible that we have to announce a few technical things or that we say something essential that has to be said. But in modern films they show you the main characters too, but after you have already arrived in the story.

At the beginning it will be strange for you, that a human being should enter the stage and just begin. But we are living in a time where people have informed themselves exactly where they go and to whom they will listen to and about which subject.

Even though you don't know this - when you took your seat, you decided to sit down for a while. Quiet please, the fun starts!

Wrong beginnings

Rearrange the audience

It can be very difficult to deliver a speech in a very big hall where are only a few people. The audience feels lost, the mood is bad and the speaker's perspective is demotivating.

Block off the seats in the back rows, if you want to make a film for example and you want the room to look full. Hire an attendant who takes care that every seat is occupied in the first rows or give everyone a numbered seat.

But if the spectators are already sitting, it is too late. Someone who is forced to change their seat often only does it reluctantly. It should be an exception to ask people to change places who have taken their seats. No one likes to give up the seat they have already chosen. Even when the first row is empty you can't remove the first row. Then people in the second row are suddenly sitting in the first row…

The structure or agenda

From my point of view this is a common mistake: Most speaker give a short overview for the audience what is to come at the beginning. Maybe it is a schedule, maybe the structure of their speech or the composition of their argumentation. Something like this:

> First of all I'd like to have a short glance into the past, then we will discuss in detail the here and now so at the end in a very brave step we will take a look into the future…

It bores them to death, because the tension is completely gone. When we talk about our holidays, we don't begin like: Let me give you a short overview over the different kind of watersports then I will describe in a few sentences our hotel and at the end will tell you about three excursions. In a good novel, things start right away.

Just as he came around the corner he knew that he would have not a single chance...

For a speech which should bring people to action, which should be exciting, which should make people interested in a subject or which introduces new scientific cognitions, an overview of the content of the speech is, from my prospective, a wrong beginning.

Structure, agenda, time table, overview... these are all valuable in a lesson. If you are holding lectures or you want to teach people something. Then your pupils love it when they can see exactly what you are intending to say. Pupils and students learn more easily with a structure and it is easier for them to connect to something they already know when they are very sure what will be discussed.   **!**

A fanfare

Some speakers love music for their appearance. At a fair for example, when there is no MC it can be very helpful to be announced with music. I am often asked what kind of music I would like at the beginning of my performance.

But be careful with too much emotionalism. If the melody of "Star Wars" can be heard or the trumpets of Jericho together with the Vienna philharmonic orchestra, then you have to fill the expectations. If something really extraordinary doesn't follow, you as a speaker are the first disappointment of the evening. The more bombastic the music is, the bigger the anticipation is.

Be careful with the use of music if you don't have the rights. You can't just choose the music you like and use it for your presentation. In every electronic shop, you can get a CD with music which is allowed to be played   **!**

without paying anything. But if you want to use something very special, you have to ask for permission

Entering the stage

There are actors and speakers who love the longest possible way to the stage, in order to have a big entry. American presidents love to walk with a waving hand through the audience.

Inexperienced speakers, who are afraid of entering a stage, begin to speak while they are walking towards the middle of the stage to avoid the embarrassment of the silence at the beginning.

The king and the queen of speech arrive in the middle of the stage and find their place and stand still for one moment – then he or she begins.

Getting undressed

Even when you put your hand on the button of your trousers and only the indication of getting undressed evokes a dead sure laughter in every comedy play. You also get this kind of laughter when using scatology and you swallow the word at the last moment or when you make sexist remarks.

They laugh because you dumbed it down, also people who find theses jokes disgusting laugh most of the time. Resist to those gimmicks and don't look for the laughter at all costs.

Asking for silence

Sometimes it can be helpful to get announced. But I never would begin with the wish:

Ladies and Gentlemen, may I have your attention, please!

If someone is standing in front, it is clear for everyone that he wants to speak. When the audience doesn't let him begin then here is something wrong and the spectators have a message for the speaker. Should the people simply be in good spirit and are talking to each other, then you should wait a short moment.

Avoidable beginnings

Don't clear your throat before you present. Don't think, whether or not you would prefer to rise or rest and don't glance frightenedly towards your spouse. Too late – the fun has begun. Here are a few more things you should avoid if possible:

Arranging the stage

To furnish the stage is a very important process. The place of the speaker on the stage implies a lot of non-verbal signals. Place and direction of the lectern, the table for the projector and the rotation of the flip chart I define detail-orientedly before every speech. But always before - and not when I enter the stage to begin with my speech.

Pulling up your pants

You have already done this before. Adjusting your blouse, correcting your jacket or pulling up your pants is rather unfavorable as a first impression that the audience gets from you. Many speakers prefer to adjust their clothes. Don't - at the moment everybody is looking at you, your time is running.

Drinking water

You have already experienced this before as well. And a glass of still water, which is already filled, is on the stage in case of emergency. Your mouth is only dry, when you are nervous. In a case of need bite your tongue very shortly and your mouth will fill with water, the feeling of dryness vanishes and you are not forced to drink because you have to speak.

Bothering the sound technician

The technician notices when you want to say something. You should neither speak an endless line of the word "test" nor knock on the microphone or ask whether this gadget works. Breathe in and begin.

You have the most difficulties when there is no technician at all and someone else has fixed the volume knob with tape in a position which was defined in advance. The acoustics of the room are different with spectators; speakers often speak louder when there is an audience in the room and sometimes they hold the microphone differently when the speech begins. If you want to be sure that everything is fine, someone should stay next to the sound mixer the whole time and supervise the volume of the sound if required.

!

Testing everything

Either a helper has prepared everything or you did it all by yourself. But when the action starts, your first move shouldn't lead to the remote control of your projector to click the first slide. You shouldn't even remove the ad for the hotel from the first page of your flipchart or you shouldn't test whether your felt-pen is okay. But make sure that the stairs has been tested and that no part of the stage creaks.

The universal beginning

It doesn't matter where, to whom and why you speak: The beginning for all good speeches in the world is the same. Before it really starts, it should always start as follows. And it doesn't play any role what the subject is:

1. The break

Inexperienced speakers don't wait; rather they begin their speech on the stairs already. They are afraid of the silence, when they get to center stage. They want to avoid this embarrassing moment when everybody stares at them. They want to get this over with as quickly as possible.

The professional rises from his seat very slowly, enters the platform and takes his place right in the middle of the stage. He breathes in, deeply but inaudibly and he doesn't gaze downwards. He looks at the audience. He grounds himself. He has arrived. He becomes one with the stage. Then he counts to three in his head. The audience doesn't get the reheated speech from yesterday nor are they guinea pigs for the speech of tomorrow. Today they are his counterparts. They can sense one another. He needs this special moment, when he can tune in to the crowd.

Only when he is sure that he knows what the audience wants from him at that moment, then he begins. Then he says: *Ladies and Gentlemen* or *A very warm welcome!* or *What a day!* Then he makes a short break. And then, and only then - he begins.

Improvable beginnings

2. Before I begin

Surely it can be necessary to explain something concerning your topic before it starts. However, this would be your new beginning. The first sentence is always the first sentence and therefore it is the beginning. It is very bothersome if you begin before you begin.

Before I start…

Even if you have to announce a wrongly parked car at first: That is your new start. That is the first impression you give. So you better have an idea about how to make the wrongly parked car interesting or someone else should take care that the car is parked somewhere else.

I once saw a speaker who got excited after entering the stage about the camera set up within sight. Nobody came to take the camera down and he had to go on without anything happening. But the beginning was a mess.

3. Begin at the beginning

Even if it is not logical at the first glance: a good speech never begins with the beginning. Essays begin at the beginning. Most fictional stories and adventures begin at the beginning, too. But thrilling speeches begin as thrilling stories at the point where the action starts. Maybe in the middle, maybe at the aftermath of the story. A story which is constructed to begin at the beginning is boring. Don't begin like this:

At the tender age of 12 months…

Even when I was a small school boy

Don't horrify your audience with the first sentences already. We are not interested in the whole history of computer development, when you are just presenting a new keyboard.

4. Request something

Many speakers begin their speech by explaining their intention.

At first I would like to present

First of all I will

Because of the fact that time is precious, my recommendation is to simply say what you want to say.

5. Use softener phrases

It is the same, if you know exactly what you want, but you say it in a way as if you were not certain.

I would like…

Probably we could at first…

Especially in English speaking countries it is very common, but if you only would like to do it, you don't do it, because you would do it, if they'd let you. Therefore no *I would* at the beginning or *Would you please let me…* Because you want to begin, don't you?

6. Excuse yourself

If something is not as it should be you can mention it quickly.

This presentation was planned differently

I will speak much shorter today than you expect it…

Although you can excuse yourself if there is something to apologize for, but don't be disheartened, obedient, sniveling or anxious. Mistakes happen – even you and you correct them as well as possible. But if your speech starts with an aria of excuses, it can be very boring for your audience.

I am not really the expert

The slides are not ideal, I know. Much to my regret...

I feel a little bit sheepish about it...

By the way, concerning stage fright, every excuse is inappropriate. Mention it very shortly if you will. But with a strong voice and own it. The king and the queen wouldn't excuse things they can't change. Nervousness belongs to it. Unfortunately, we can't decide whether we are nervous or not.

7. Pumping up the crowd

Posing questions during a presentation can be an effective feature to activate your audience, to create tension and to make your subject interesting. Oftentimes there is a Q&A session at the end of the speech.

But I personally hate these motivational questions at the beginning of a speech to put people in a better mood.

Are you ready? Do you like it?

Is everything well with the world?

Isn't it amazing? And now all together!

How are we all doing? We can do it better!

For the vicarious embarrassment it helps when the speaker puts really a lot of pressure in his questions and shouts at the audience.

On the other hand when everybody is nearly drunk then I probably would like to change my mind. But even then you could have another idea as

Do you feel alright? I want to hear a YES!

8. Giving commands

Nothing is more stressful for your audience than constantly being yelled at, what to buy next, what to do next or what you have to believe from now on, especially not at the beginning.

> *You have to believe me one thing!*

> *You will change your life from now on!*

> *I will help you here and now to a happier future!*

I doubt whether people change their behavior when you shout the solutions at them.

> *More fun in live, less weight, happier employees!*

> *Do something for your career!*

These are all beginnings where I would cross my internal arms and think: *Ok, do it! I am very curious whether you are successful.* And in this case it is not meant in a positive way. The speaker should take care when trying to convince me.

24

Classical beginnings

Everybody begins like this. Therefore when you want to use a classical beginning, you should think it over a second time. Not because these beginnings are bad, but because we have already heard everything. And you can only get attention with otherness or strangeness. You can only express individuality when you don't follow the mainstream.

If there is no other way and you are sure that you want a classical beginning, because for example in your company everyone uses the same opener, then nevertheless you could try to put the classical beginnings at the second or third place of your speech.

Begin with something thrilling, something surprising. Followed by the point you wanted to use originally as a beginning. Grip our audience from the first moment on. Don't bother me with opener phrases I have already heard countless times.

Of course you are allowed to shout *A very warm welcome* to the crowd, when the public swimming pool opens after five years of construction for the first time. Of course you are allowed to speak about the honor to hold this speech by proxy of the prime minister. If you make a joke and the effect is, that everybody flips out their mobile device then you are even allowed to begin with questioning the mobile phone. If you have an idea, even a classical beginning can be a good beginning. It only has to be different. A few thoughts on this subject:

9. A warm welcome

A *warm welcome* as the first speaker is ok. With a genuine smile and a serious subline, that means with a friendly melody, this can be a very good opening. But didn't you already say hello to everyone? And if not, are you really the first speaker? Didn't your predecessor welcome everybody and say hello to everyone?

If you repeat it, this can be very tedious for the audience. A common bad habit is, to wish *a warm welcome* when you are the third or fourth speaker. Varied by *a warm welcome of myself* or *may I take the chance to welcome you.* And if you hear the word welcome after 12pm again, you'll scream. A professional speaker doesn't do this.

A professional has still some other idea. And that is not *Good morning, Good evening* or *Good night*. For example it is likeable to say

> *How wonderful that so many friends have time to celebrate with me on a Tuesday evening.*

> *That is especially true for the colleagues who haven't been here. Great that you got to know "our" hotel right now.*

> *I am happy about every single person who has come to us today.*

If you privately say Hello to your guests you don't say *A warm welcome* to 60 people with the same intonation, but you invent a lot of variations to give every guest the feeling that he is meant and no one else.

But if the professional use a warm welcome one time, then he uses a well prepared subline, a mixture of *Nice to have you here* and *I am feeling very well.*

10. A greeting

A good opening is tailored to the event. The audience wants to hear that the speaker is with them today. Especially so for the professionals who speak very often and who are in a different city every day. The audience wants to be sure that the speaker is ware of their town, their hall, their company. Instead of *Nice to have you here!* it should sound as concrete as possible.

Wonderful that you came to Cologne

Welcome to Lessing Street!

Instead of *Ladies and gentlemen y*ou could again say it much more concrete:

Today they are here: Customers, Employees...

Everyone you came tonight is called a friend of mine.

So it sounds more personal. Or you skip the greeting for the time being. Or you postpone it. If you can listen to the lowest noise here is still time to be delighted because so many people showed up.

11. Introducing yourself

Most speakers begin this way. Despite the name of the speaker being on the first page of the invitation, every mail being signed by the speaker and a big portrait of him showing on the huge slide in the back of the stage in blinking letters, most of the speakers first explain who they are. That is not only superfluous. Sometimes it is even disgusting.

If you, however, want to begin this way, because you think it is absolutely necessary then take care that your self-introduction is extraordinary or surprising. Maybe you don't explicitly begin with the name...

Most of you know who I am. But only a few of you know what I do.

Even the argument that it would be impolite not to introduce heself, it is totally superfluous, an interesting opening is possible. Or you at least keep it quite short. The speaker and trainer Margit Hertlein recommends introducing oneself with a triad:

> *At the same time I am an Alfa Romeo Cabriolet, a VW-Minibus and a truck.*

> *Speaker, actor, trainer. And additionally I am someone who makes things different.*

As soon as it sounds different we listen carefully and you have our full attention.

> *They call me the fire brigade for the vibes!*

> *I am the one who is called from desperate CEOs when they don't know how to go further.*

If you do it like this even a boring introduction can be rather thrilling for the audience.

12. Feeling honoured

If it is really an honor to speak at this hour at this place then you should say this. If you are really surprised that you have been chosen as a speaker, you may take this as a subject. But again please avoid the usual wording which tells us something about how unimaginative the speaker is, like:

> *Today I have the honor…*

> *May I thank you for the honor…*

You could do this much more personal

> *When Mr. Important asked me, whether I like to speak today, I was very much appreciated.*

> *It's an honor for me that especially you invited me to speak…*

> *You have chosen me for this speech. Thank you!*

Needless to say that the joy has to be genuine, the humility has to be honest and the respect has to be serious.

13. Asking for permission

Many speakers ask for permission to speak first. I don't know whether it is false politeness or ritualized respect. But if you scrutinize the sentences regarding their content, they do sound a little bit funny.

Let me shortly

May I very shortly at the beginning

If you allow...

Please give me the opportunity...

The king doesn't ask everyone for permission whether he is now really allowed to speak. If you really have to ask for permission to speak, because your boss is ill or you only got time to speak after a long period of pleading, then you can say thank you for the opportunity.

It was not so easy to get the allowance to speak here tonight.

I allow myself to do it a little bit different today

But to simply feel around very careful whether you are allowed, should, could, probably want... you can skip this passage without substitution.

14. Saying thank you

For your audience a long eulogy with thank you to all and everyone is very annoyed and bored. The amateur at the beginning says thanks for everything good which has been done to him in the last two weeks. He says thank you to the technician for using the volume knob, thank you to his predecessor for the nice words and thank you to the host of the event for the invitation and thank you to the audience that they will let him speak. It sounds like this…

> *Thank you Mr. Major, thank you to our priest and a special thank you to my predecessor and thank you to you Ladies and Gentlemen for coming.*

Not even the persons you are mentioned are happy about this kind of thanks. If it must be good then it should always be more than saying thank you. Try saying thanks batter using phrases which no speaker has used before.

> *He doesn't like it if I mention him…*

> *At first I will say thank you to him that I will never forget…*

The nicest thank you is personally and unmistakably connected to the person you want to thank.

> *How many times did we meet to prepare today's event*

It is important to say thank you. There is no discussion. But again it is a question of the right moment and the way you do it. Maybe you don't choose the beginning and say thank you with a very special idea, so that it is a pleasure even for people who don' know the person you say thank you to.

> *With her left hand she ate a portion of French fries while she was typing invitation lists with her right hand…*

Simply the fact that you did recognize that she very often skipped lunch for you will make your secretary happy.

15. Guests of Honour

Sometimes you don't have the choice whether you to say thank you to a few persons or not. Sometimes it has to be done. Possibly you say thank you to the CEO of the local bank when you mention your charity project. And you say thank you to the best wife of all when you are talking about the time you spend with his event. To say thank you a few times in between is not iresome for the audience, moreover, it can be very entertaining.

But aren't there some speaking formats where you have to begin with an address of welcome? Yes, if you say something personal, concrete and not exchangeable the mentioning of the honored guests can be a lot of fun for the audience.

He doesn't like to go to events

He just came from Hamburg where he attended a big convention...

f you want to be extraordinary good, you can tell us something about today's very special meeting.

It may not be the most important part of the evening for you. But it is for me. I fought two years that he is with us tonight. I had a lot of phone calls and I had to be very charming

f you don't have any information then you can talk to your honored guest at the beginning of your meeting. Even a sentence ike

He just told me

When she arrived...

s a personal beginning which can transport a piece of nformation which might be valuable for the audience.

Be careful with the sequence of honorary guests. The order s fixed and there are certain rules for official meetings which you shouldn't break...

!

31

16. Being delighted

If it is not a set phrase you can be very glad that so many people attend this meeting. But you shouldn't use a formulation which everyone uses in this situation like:

I very much appreciate that so many people...

And there are even openers which are a little bit out of fashion.

I am very glad that you have found your way to our event.

What a silly sentence in the time of sat navs! This sounds ridiculous. Our sat nav even tells us the right side of the street. Better use a sentence which hasn't been overused. Our joy is different and we all use totally different sentences to express how glad we are. Let's assume that there are really many more spectators than you originally thought. And that makes you happy!

Believe me, from the stage the crowd looks even bigger...

How lucky that we put a few more chairs in the room...

As long as the phrase which expresses your delight is not interchangeable, everything is fine.

17. A foreign language

Implementing a foreign language is always a gift for people who speak this language. It is a question of appreciation. Saying hello in different languages is a wonderful beginning, although it is a classical beginning.

Buongiorno, guten Morgen, buenos dias! I should actually like to welcome you in eight different languages, because so many nations are here today.

Mesdames, Messieurs, bienvenue! A welcome from the heart to our French guests.

32

was told that a speech in China works much better when you say something in Cantonese or in Mandarin. And it doesn't matter how skilled you are.

Content beginnings

Most speakers begin with the content, if they start at all. They speak about their subject. They tell us what they are talking about. But very often, not before they have wished a warm welcome, said thank you, led to the issue, felt honored, pleaded for permission or expressed their delight.

My recommendation is to jump into your subject right away. You don't begin the story of your holiday with you packing suitcases but always where the action starts. For example with the two meter-long shark in the water near the beach or about your luggage which didn't follow you to your destination.

18. A personal story

It is obvious that a story is a wonderful opportunity to get attention. My recommendation is to begin with it without a preamble.

> *Imagine three young men, with enough money from their parents in their pockets and the unstoppable will to make a life-changing experience.*

Or when you introduce a product or project.

> *I will never forget the moment when the idea arose to possibly take a complete other way to succeed...*

Such a personal story has an additional advantage: A beginning like that is not difficult. You lived through the story and it is easy to talk about.

19. A story from others

The internet is full of stories. When you are browsing social networks you will be provided accordingly. And when you lik story very much it doesn't matter that some people know it. Like this joke for example.

In Munich, a department store for husbands has recently opened, and at the entrance there is a manual explaining the rules according to which shopping can be done here: There are six floors with men whose characteristics improve from floor to floor. You can go further up, but you can't go back to a lower floor.

But skip the sultan in the Middle East who travelled with his three donkeys... That may be a little bit more modern. If you read a good newspaper you only have to collect a little bit to find a good current story which suits your subject.

A doctor from Syria enters a German pharmacy and wants...

Please, no stories about Steve Jobs and Richard Branson. Not even from Kodak or Google. Nobody can listen to them for the next ten years. (Except if your story is brand new!)

You can even begin with a well-known story. But then it has to be short and right to the point. No introduction, no dramaturgy of tension, no chronology: In the story about the tortoise and the hare, why does the tortoise always win the race? The answer is simple...

20. A home-made fairy-tale

You can guess now that it has to begin with „Once upon a time.." and then it should continue very modern and contemporary. This is also a very simple way to alter a clear subject into a picture so that people will listen to you.

Once upon a time there was a little smartphone that nobody wanted to buy. And the people, who had manufactured it, were rather sad about it...

Once upon a time there were three men at the height of their life. They were looking for a distraction…

It is a little bit more difficult to rewrite a well-known fairytale to adapt it to the occasion of the event.

The question is here: Who is Snow-white and who are the seven dwarves?

Little red riding hood looks a little bit different in our company…

Fairy-tales are so widespread that we recognize them instantly. Without too much explanation it is clear for everyone what the message is.

For the birthday of a girl friend I once wrote a fairytale where a fairy offers her to turn back time. The question was: To which age? Of course the punchline was that she wanted to stay exactly as old as she had just become.

21. Looking behind the scenes

In artificial English you would say: Deliver a few pieces of background information. Tell the audience what they couldn't possibly know. Let them be a part of the creative process of your speech.

14 people have been working towards today's success for a whole year. We left nothing to chance and met very, very often. The number of cups of coffee is in the four-digit range. We wanted to have the best experts on the subject here. And we succeeded.

Sometimes it is also possible that something has happened shortly before that results in a very exciting start.

This morning at 9am I got a call from the fire department that this event could not take place as we planned it.

or this opening you won't have much time for preparation, because you could not know weeks in advance what will happen at the day of your event. But these are only examples. And I change the opening of my speech often minutes before I begin, as long as I stay with my personal topics and stories, this is not so difficult.

It was during the afternoon of a stressful strategy-meeting. We were tired and had no results. Then Titus came up with the idea to use a special creativity technique that he had just heard about...half an hour later we were outbidding each other with ideas.

This small look behind the scenes, which none of your spectators can normally do, is something very exciting. Mostly there are experts on stage, and it doesn't matter whether they are experts for the spiritual life of the birthday boy or experts for the product or service we are talking about. When these experts give us some pieces of insider information, then it can be a very good beginning.

22. Giving a statement

Why not begin your speech with an argument? Define something. Put a clear claim at the beginning of your speech. However, such a proposition at the beginning is only a good opener if it is provocative or unexpected or totally unfamiliar to the audience.

For me good communication is not the training of the right sentences or following the rules. For me good communication is as individual as the people who are involved.

Such a beginning is not an offer to talk and there is some kind of bite, but a lot of situations come to my mind where this sharpness is appropriate.

A school event in the middle of the week? Only over my dead body!

A salary raise of 2 percent is ridiculous.

I will say it loud and clear: Especially because of the discussion yesterday: A better prize winner could not have been found.

The French speaker and trainer Francis Zentz began a meeting for sales-people with

If you do sales for twenty years, then you're somehow more open.

This was a big laughter. These beginnings have the big advantage that they lead us right up to our subject. The listeners get a feeling of your dynamism.

23. A (scientific) cognition

If you don't just use the Gallup-study (not because it's bad, but because everyone uses it) you can evoke a lot of curiosity and increase their awareness with some scientific investigations.

The average age of mankind all over the world in the year 1950 was 23 years old, in the year 2005 it had already increased to 28 years old. It stems from this that our birthday girl is older than the average.

The more the cognition has to do with the topic the better. And the cognition has not to be necessarily scientific.

We asked 500 secretaries what makes them angry or bothers them most at work. How do you think they responded? No, it is not a lack of acknowledgement from their boss...

A nice collection of articles from the newspapers' science page can be a good treasure trove for well booked speakers. And if you

ead books then take notes what inspires you. Only wisdom that
you retain can be harnessed.

24. Something surprising

The memory expert, Markus Hofmann, begins his speeches along
he lines of:

> *At the end of my speech you will be excited. Not by me, that
> could also be. But you will be excited about yourself.*

The probability that your curiosity is piqued is comparatively
high. I begin my speeches very often with this thought:

> *To be honest, I shouldn't be here. I don't teach anything.
> You can't learn anything from me, what you don't even
> know. My subject is making features disappear.*

As long as your audience is attentive because of something
unexpected, anything is allowed. Only a wobbly chair gets
attention. If the chair you are sitting on is not wobbling you won't
find him the next day among hundreds of other chairs.

Tell us something which is exceptional and your audience will
remember your speech for days on end. Scrutinize your topic for
the fact that most people will suggest it is quite the opposite. This
is the material for a good start.

25. Revealing a secret

Secrets obviously grab attention. Begin with just that.

> *Could you imagine that someone like me was very afraid of
> walking on stage tonight? Afraid of you, afraid of the huge
> technical equipment, afraid of failure.*

I know that many trainers don't recommend beginning with
something negative. But for me the overcoming of fear isn't
something negative. As long as you are not tearful and whiny-

voiced there is no reason not to talk about your anxieties
Admitting your own fear makes you approachable and this is just
the way to show strength.

> *Ladies and gentlemen, this is my last day. The last day of*
> *this project and my last day in this department. Luckily not*
> *the last day in the company.*

If nobody is prepared for this secret, it can be a very strong
beginning. Even if there was not a future for me in this company
I would begin my farewell speech like this. First state the clear
facts and while everyone is probably shocked or puzzled, you can
explain and help your audience cope with the situation.

26. Rhetorical questions

Rhetorical questions are a very old and, even among the oldest
of Greeks, a tad bit overused technique. Maybe the reason is that
everybody understands this figure of speech at once and it is easy
as pie to implement. Nevertheless, a question is something
activating, because everybody then reflects on a possible
response. Even if they doesn't have a chance to give an answer.

> *Do we all know what the person celebrating a jubilee might*
> *have done if we weren't here?*

> *How often have we asked whether or not we are right with*
> *our new strategy?*

During my speeches I very often ask questions to which I want
to have the answers. But never at the beginning.

Firstly, the speaker has to gain the trust of the audience. They
have to learn that nothing extraordinary will happen if they
answer questions.

There are many speakers who trick or con the audience or prove
that the audience has no clue at all, unlike the speaker. But
rhetorical question at the beginning is not a problem.

Honestly? Do you like being here?

Why do you think we invited you here today?

often ask questions which are not rhetorical but actual questions.

What do you do if you were angry?

What is the hot topic at your dinner table?

But my answer is so quick that the participants have no chance to reply. The reason is that I don't want to lose speed. If every member of the audience says something at the beginning, the tension curve declines to zero. Sometimes it has to go on without waiting for detail oriented answers.

Furthermore, I can't control the answers. If I get an answer everybody is waiting for it will be boring. If I get answers which am not expecting, in the worst case, I will stammer and everything else which is coming suddenly will become much more complicated.

27. Reading something out loud

Free speech and reading? Yes, these go together. I am not talking about the text of your speech (you should know it). But maybe you discovered something in a book, a newspaper or a brochure of a local company, maybe very shortly before your speech. Because you haven't learnt it by heart, you just read it.

I just found a headline in the local newspaper, which expresses exactly...

The presenter and speaker Denise Maurer once began by coming on stage with a pile of newspapers she had just been given by an elderly lady on the train. Then she read out what she had noticed in connection to the event.

41

At a big event I found a brochure from the inviting organization hours before the start. I stumbled upon a very complicated sentence with lots of nouns and parentheses in an almost caricatured language. I read this article at the beginning of the speech and the effect was a big laughter without any explanation. This was the subject: Outside the organization no member of the community will be properly understood.

> *After the school final examination comes an apprenticeship, then academic studies, then a temporary employment abroad, then academic studies again, four internships in total and then again an apprenticeship. It seems as...*

Especially when it becomes complicated with titles, technical language and special profession terms, it is important to be accurate: Just read it! And if you do it right at the beginning one of the biggest difficulties of your speech has already been managed.

28. Looking into the future

Obeying the rules of many trainers, the look into the future would be the end of a speech. For this reason it is thrilling to begin with such an outlook.

> *In 20 years employees will no longer search for companies but companies will fight for every single employee.*

> *65 percent of all professions that will be taken up by those who are currently attending primary school do not yet exist. Drone operator, tele-policeman...*

This works even if your vision of the future is speculative. As long as you are getting attention, everything is okay.

> *The bank of the future is in my imagination still in the center of the city. A lot of people are working in the lobby.*

But all the technical procedures will be done by machines. Bank statement printers are completely useless…

If we meet again in two years then one subject will occupy almost everyone

Either positive or negative, thinking about the future engages us all and grabs our attention. You don't have to be a futurologist to put the unknown in the center of attention.

Linguistic beginnings

29. A metaphor

Painting a beautiful linguistic picture is something very effective
At its best it weaves a thread throughout the whole speech. Such
a metaphor provides the audience with a new point of view and
shows how you can make an interesting twist on subjects which
are very often discussed.

> *He doesn't blow with the wind but he is a strong wind
> generator in the North Sea which supports the whole
> department with energy.*

A time ago I met a team leader who was a big fan of the TV series
"Star Trek". The subject of his speech was that his own team is
not the guys in the machine room but the ones sitting on the
bridge of the space craft, right next to commander Kirk. This was
very demonstrative.

> *On our cemetery of ideas there will be a new funeral.*

> *Let's put the rose colored glasses away!*

> *I don't go over this bridge, I don't drive over this crossing,
> I don't enter this ship…*

> *If your text is a printer's nightmare, you don't have to
> wonder whether the reader will get scared.*

Caution: No more sailing ships. Not a single brochure
about financial products without ships, not a single boss
who uses the slack period to motivate his team and no Billy
the Kid who doesn't like to sail against the wind. Also
regarding the metaphor of a group of mountaineers - I
would take a second look…

!

30. A comparison

This is a very easy way to get an impressive beginning, too. Robert Spengler, a rhetoric and communication trainer does it like this:

Your presentation has to be like an espresso: strong, intense and flavorful.

The boss of a big German bank was the third speaker on a meeting of executives. He was bored to death while listening so he looked outside the window and his gaze went to the big meadows around the building. Then he finally began:

Isn't management a little bit like cutting the grass? A thought just dawned on me that...

Such comparisons are very easy to find. When you use a metaphor throughout the whole speech, a lot of impressive pictures can be created.

31. A slogan or saying

If you use a sound slogan as an introduction, it shouldn't be something that is being treasured for the next generation. The sound bite should not have a double meaning or contain a funny pun, but most people who deliver speeches have a motto. My slogan is

Become as you are!

Companies have slogans, too, which lead to a great beginning for your speech.

Everyone has something that propels him.

German Speakers Association – everything a speaker needs.

But you can also create such a sound bite about your subject by yourself.

> *It doesn't matter when, where or what - important is that we do it together.*

> *When charm was for sale he shouted "Here!" three times.*

The sound bite can even be a little bit longer. It only has to explain in short terms what you are talking about today.

> *Projects come and go. If something should stay forever you shouldn't go when it comes.*

Inspiring is such an adage, almost as if it had a certain easiness. Quotes which you hammer with a lot of emphasis onto the head of your participants are only stressful.

32. A rhyme

I know that rhymes are a little bit frumpy, as if they were out of style. But this is not true if they are brilliant. A bad rhyme is something to be ashamed of, except when it is a joke. But you can turn a simple statement with a rhyme very easily into a very good adage.

> *And suddenly it dawned on you – it is true!*

> *What do we learn from this? – The beginning is a kiss.*

> *A case is a case. Two cases are a trace.*

There was a very good speech from the spokesperson of a big insurance company which began with this quote. They wanted to make clear that in a certain area of the company something was wrong.

If the speech is private it can also be a little bit foolish. But only if you like that kind of stuff.

> *May be it's just me - that we got beer instead of tea.*

With Bee we were three.

Want to wear some belly jeans, better eat more jelly beans.

f you create your own rhymes, take care that the word that doesn't suit that well comes first. Then the bad word doesn't stand out so much.

If you like to fell a tree, try it in our company.

The biggest trouble I ever had was with my dad.

It happened by the sea – naturally.

If you are a mover – look for Vancouver!

t gets more modern when you start rapping. I once experienced how a professional rapper summarized the content of an event n rhymes - simply great. Rhyming can be quite modern.

33. A play on words

Everything which is funny, provocative or surprising is allowed. You want the attention from the first moment on. How can it go asier than with an expression or a quote which does not yet xist?

How can we go into something when we don't go to someone?

A flipchart with empty pencils is a flopchart.

n easy way to invent new words is making up words with a ouble meaning.

You can't drive a racing heart.

When you look at the word team, there is an „I am" in it.

peaker Frans Reinhardt started his presentation at a Dutch peaker Convention with

A penis!

That was the answer of a woman when she was asked about the most important thing in life. But the woman was French, who spoke English with a strong accent. Actually she wanted to say "happiness"!

If you don't have any idea you only have to make a short journey through the endless vastness of the internet. You will be surprised, what you can find, clearly arranged around different topics.

34. A made up word

First you look at expressions which have to do with your subject. Then you try to change these expressions a little bit so that you create a new word which hasn't existed until now.

I am Powerpointologist.

Pia is deinstructable.

The first spacecraft with four wheels.

Begin to program a meditation- manager!

Insurance was yesterday. Today it is called withsurance.

A thesaurus can be very helpful, when combining words or parts of words which have never have been connected into a new word. Or you look for words which sound similar, and then change them.

Do you know a Vegeterrorist? No? I don't mean a vegetoxic or a vegetarget.

The Austrian speaker Ulrike Aichhorn in her speeches talks about learning "kundinisch", a word that is derived from the word "Kundin", a German word meaning a female customer.

Or have you ever heard the word Complexitation? Two examples from the annual meeting of the national speakers association in America:

Are we people or sheeple?

Do you know what a nearling is? (www.nearling.com)

Such a word is not easy to find. Take a sheet of paper and a pencil with you to the gym or when you are jogging. On a long journey with your car a dictaphone or smartphone in the center console is a perfect aid when creating a new word.

35. Quotes

Using quotes is not very groundbreaking, I admit. During my rhetoric lessons I would never allow you to begin with a quote, especially when it is from Shaw, Churchill or Lincoln. But there are so many very good sayings, which can be used for an opener. I have been collecting for 30 years now…

If everything seems under control, you're not going fast enough. (Mario Andretti, American race car driver)

Action is the antidote to despair. (Joan Baez)

My death will open your eyes. (Margit Hertlein)

Or you know some cool sentence. Or you cite your mother, a colleague, who has said something very wise or remarkable. My teacher at acting school Ruth v. Zerboni always said

If you sit, your bum is your feet.

I will never forget this sentence, because it is so catchy. But avoid expressions like

A wise man once said…

How did Cicero just say?

The saying and mentioning the name of the author is enough. In case of Margit Hertlein you can ad that she is a speaker. But there is seldom time for long introductions.

36. Arranged quotes and sayings

It would be even better, if you changed a famous sentence in such a way that we listen again. In that case the sentence can even be very famous.

There is no place like the next pub.

Ask not what you can do for your country, ask what you can do for your spouse!

Where these sentences come from doesn't matter. Maybe they are sentences from a commercial or very old sayings. It is only important that the original saying is still recognizable. Otherwise the listeners have less fun.

Don't put all your legs in one basket!

We kill one bird with five stones!

I was head over high heels in love!

It works just as well for a lecture at the company.

The early bird catches the market!

A golden app can open any door!

First bosses first.

With a little bit of creativity this is the first joke of the evening.

When Mia is away, her husband will pay.

In this case changing, copying and inspiration are allowed. You don't have to invent the wheel a second time, but you should be creative.

37. Quotes from commercials

The easiest way to find quotes and sayings is to look at commercials. If the commercial is well known a short hint will be enough to make your audience smile, because they understand.

Just do it. – And we did it!

It's not a Sony. But it is the best shaver in the world.

Feel the difference! And look at the difference!

The fun increases when you change the saying from the commercial a little bit more to make it fit to the event or to your speech.

Bido – the world's favorite punchline.

Our host – practically magic!

The Walldorf Astoria – because we are worth it.

You see, that the most interesting thing is the wrapping. A simple "Thank you" to express that the event is taking place at the Walldorf Astoria in New York is not funny, but linking it to an L'Oreal slogan could make your audience smile.

38. The news

Your speech could begin like the news on TV. One short sentence at the beginning and the setup is made.

Gräfelfing. Preparations are in full swing for today's birthday party at the home of the Rossié- family.

Nottingham. 62 managers meet to celebrate and work together.

Maybe the subject is something we would like to hear, but nobody is talking about it because the things aren't as they should be.

> *Birmingham. After a few difficulties at the beginning the SUPER AG is looking upon a very successful year. CEO Dr.Power emphasized that the common efforts...We wouldn't have got these news in the last year, because it didn't look good for our company.*

For a good friend I began a speech on his birthday party by reading out loud an imaginary article from the local newspaper. In the typical style of an article I read what a newspaper might have said about him.

39. Telegram style

Especially when a story is longer, telegram style can help you come right to the point. The story is accelerated a lot and this is the direct road to the attention of the participants. They decide during the first minutes, whether they prefer to let their mind wander to a canoe tour down the Amazonas river instead.

> *Saturday night. Shortly after 10pm. I see a light in the teacher's room. Whom will I meet? Gudrun. She is tidying up. For hours. Her comment: I could do this the whole weekend.*

Or an example for the introduction of a new product.

> *Monday, 23rd of January. Beads of perspiration on our foreheads. The 18th attempt. Again nothing. The mechanism failed. Again. Allas, we had the idea which changed everything.*

Such a short and forward – pressing introduction increases the tension in each case. Every new concept has a story of its development. Even a prize winner was discovered at a certain minute. We have all first heard of a new idea at a certain time and place.

40. A trick question

Whether you use a trick question only for laughter or to lead to your subject is up to you.

Why was I born in Texas? - Well, my mother wanted to be with me!

How many of you learned blind typing? – I not interested in the answer at all, but I do think this is a good opener!

You can replace the capability of blind typing with anything else and the joke also works.

You know that look women get when they want sex? Me neither. (Drew Carey)

Here you will very quickly find another redraft, which suits to your topic, too. Simply look at some trick questions. With a little bit of creativity there are a bunch of punchline possible, which henceforth belong to you. And messing around with the audience is just a very good beginning. There a still a few variations. Imagine your company produces refrigerators...

Do you know what the perfect fridge looks like? Gotcha! I expected this. This is the reason why we aren't assembling it already.

For such a kind of joke you have to have a special kind of affection. If you are only grinning tiredly at my examples the trick question is the wrong beginning for you. Cross out the chapter trick questions in your repertoire. Only that which suits you brings you the sympathy of the audience. You will find at least 99 other possibilities in this book.

!

Personal beginnings

41. About the place

An opening which suits any speech has certain advantages. But there is one thing you will not achieve: The participants will never get the idea that they are addressed. Especially among speakers it is very important to give an audience exactly this feeling. The easiest way is to implement place and time in the beginning of your speech. In the north of Germany I once began like this:

> *In Munich we have bicycles, too. But there aren't as many bicycles as in Oldenburg. This afternoon I nearly caused two accidents. And in both cases...*

Collect what you hear and see. If it at all possible, I take a walk around the town or in the surroundings of the place of the event and I absorb everything I can find.

> *Do you know what the subject at our table at lunch was?*

> *Diagonal to our hall there is a stand-up display of an insurance company with the quote: Please, feel free to phone us! So please don't phone, if you don't feel free. In psychology this is called...*

Everyone who passes this stand-up display after the speech will smile and think about you and what you said.

Also peppermints on every desk, a kind lady at the reception, a quick technical team or a well-equipped dressing room can deliver material for a good beginning.

In the Kleist-City Frankfurt on the Oder I began with a quote which I found on the window of the public library.

> *"Nowhere can one get to know the degree of the culture of a city, and even the spirit of its dominant taste, faster and*

likewise more correctly than in the reading libraries." I just passed by it. It was chockful.

often use beginnings which anchor the speech with place and time of the presentation before the opener I have prepared. Such beginnings impress most when they build a connection to something which has just happened.

!

42. About the time

Again the subject is to give the audience the feeling that the presentation is not interchangeable. A sentence about politics (which naturally has to fit to the subject of the speech) is not usable one week later. Because the audience has just read the same news as you, a certain closeness arises.

During the last weeks before the elections you probably have listened to so many talk shows that you are tired of them. But one thing was very interesting...

It is not necessarily politics. I once held a speech on a Tuesday. On Wednesday was the first episode of The Bachelor on TV. And I began along the lines of...

I am so glad that it isn't Wednesday today. Otherwise this room would be half empty. Right? What's the matter tomorrow? Yes, tomorrow most of you will watch...

After this Key-note I got the annoying mail from a doctor who didn't feel taken seriously. He didn't watch such series and also didn't like people who watch such series. For him I had got the wrong start

If Germany has just become European soccer champion, if a celebrity has died or summer time changed to winter time, you could mention this.

43. A personal thought

As useful as it is to address the thoughts of the audience, it can be just as useful to utter your own thoughts at a beginning of a speech.

I've hesitated a long time about how to begin. How I should explain how important this project is for our company and how...

If you reveal your thoughts during preparation of the event or those right now regarding the world, the audience or your subject, they can be a wonderful bridge to your audience.

When I watch a speech or a broadcast about the future I already know what will come next: Demographic change, change management, social media... the whole package. Is this really that important?

The probability that your audience will find themselves in your thoughts is very high. Especially when they are waiting for struggles, such a beginning can be the first choice.

Are you aware that you are known as a very difficult audience?

When I prepared this speech I was very sure that you will probably think...

Such a beginning needs a big portion of self-confidence, but it's going to have a great effect. You can win the attention of your audience from the first moment on, by expressing which thoughts are currently running through your head.

44. A personal feeling

It is very gutsy to begin with your own feelings, but it is also the easiest beginning imaginable. Your feelings are always there waiting to be expressed. Which feelings do you have? Joy would be great, as would pride or satisfaction. But also skepticism or doubt are possible. Uncertainty works as well as a lack of self-assurance.

Today I don't have the courage to begin like I normally begin...

If you are now thinking, as many of the participants in my seminars do, that you, the speaker, are not important but the subject of your speech is, I must contradict vividly. If I, the listener, think you are approachable I am much more likely in a mood to deal with your subject, even if I have a contradictory opinion. You as a person are very essential for the success of your speech. Why not begin with your personal feelings? A minister of education once began a speech on a big meeting for teachers like this:

When my friends asked me to which meeting I will go today and I replied: To the teachers' meeting in Smalltown! They were really astonished. "What? You have the guts to go there?" – "Yes", I answered, "I have the guts. If we don't talk about our conflicts of opinion, we will never..."

The audience was very puzzled about the directness and it was so quiet you could have heard a pin drop.

Or sometimes I am announced as a language trainer not as a speaking trainer.

Yes, I was just a little bit frightened. If I really were a language trainer, we would have to train German now...

Or the CEO of the local bank is a little bit of a show-off with the announcement of my speech and praises the speaker a little too much.

After such an announcement I totally don't know how to begin. Thank you so much.

Sometimes minutes before my speech I even put a very persona[l]
beginning in front of the first thought of my speech.

45. The reason why you are here

I found this tip in a book written by the speaker Thoma[s]
Skipwith. Talk about the reason why you are the right person t[o]
speak about this subject. Very often this is done by the MC or th[e]
host of the event. If he doesn't do it, it can be reasonable to do i[t]
yourself.

Why do I talk about this subject? Because I have worked in
the robotics research department. for 10 years now

We've talked a lot today about in-flight security. I once sat
in a plane with 169 passengers on board, that nearly
crashed down. .

I have just arrived from Tibet...

This also works at a private meeting.

Maybe you wonder why the ex-boyfriend of the bride is
taking the microphone...

Thomas asked me to give a short speech.

That does not necessarily have something to do wit[h]
egocentrism. As an actor who talks about communication I ofte[n]
use the opportunity to develop a good start from this tension.

Now the actor comes. I know the thoughts running through
your head: What's going on? But it is different than you
think. I won't explain to you how to act, I'll do exactly the
opposite. I'll show you how useless it is if you behave like
an actor in everyday life.

Sometimes a profession has to be explained, sometimes th[e]
origin of something, perhaps the age or the (missing) educatio[n]

t can be very thrilling to explain why, of all people, you have been invited and which connection you have to the subject.

The audience will pay much more attention, if they know that the speaker has done the survey by himself or if he has really seen all the countries he is talking about or if he has worked in this special profession for decades. Then one is likely to enjoy listening to them a little bit more.

46. Poke fun at yourself

Many comedians poke fun at themselves and therefore make us laugh. A speaker can use this practise, too. I find someone more approachable, who doesn't take himself too seriously.

> *You may think that the last speech of the day would be the highlight. But to be honest: We drew straws. Nobody had the guts to hold the closing speech.*

There is no place for self-pity. In this case they shouldn't really have drawn straws.

> *Can you say „no“ when Ute begs you to hold a speech?*
> *Can you say that you are neither funny nor entertaining?*
> *Can you say that you don't have any clue what to talk about? No! If Ute asks you to hold a little speech, then you accept and you think about how to survive it afterwards.*

Because the subject is Ute at the same time, the transition is very easy. The speaker and expert for body language, Stefan Verra, pokes fun at the beginning of his speech on his lack of height. He is announced by a very bloomy voice over, and then he enters the stage and says:

> *Now you have heard: ... ten-thousand people, university teacher... and then you see ME and you think: what? This guy? This can't possibly be! And this is exactly what body language is.*

The audience was highly entertained.

47. Dialect

You have to speak the dialect very well. Imitation doesn't count. But when you show your audience that you talk like them it is a special kind of appreciation.

Howzit? (South African)

See y'all 'round! (Texan)

In most cases, all of your listeners are on your side if you are interested in your audience. And most notably when you are really a member of their group.

Be careful with dialects which you don't speak since childhood. If you use only one expression from another region or country everybody pardons the fact that it doesn't sound natural because this isn't your mother tongue and you are using this term for the first time in your life. Detail oriented expeditions in dialects which are not your own is not something I would recommend. If you make a fool of yourself, it is very difficult to be taken seriously in the following speech.

!

Again and again I am astonished at how people radiate with joy just because you come from the same area or town or if you have a contact in common. Even reading the same newspaper can evoke a feeling of connection. This can be very useful for the speaker.

Audience oriented beginnings

How about drawing attention to your audience right off the bat. At very many speeches the spectators are the real center of the event because they have paid for their tickets or because they have to be convinced.

48. Create sympathy

This tip is from the thrilling book of Matthias Nöllke "Starke Worte – einfach eine gute Rede halten". He recommends that we show the audience how much we like them. Because sympathy normally evokes empathy.

> *I was so keen on meeting you because the subject I am talking about is just...*

> *From my perspective this day could last much, much longer because I am connecting very well to you.*

As so many of the tips in this book it is very important to be concrete. Only mentioning that this is the best audience you ever had will only provoke a tired smile.

> *Such a great audience in such a great location with great food in a great mood...*

The worst thing of all at this time would be to look into the future.

> *I'm sure that you'll listen very well when I tell you...*

It is better to skip this because it also has to be true. If you don't know your audience or if you don't really like them, then it would be advisable to choose another beginning.

49. Reading the mind of your audience

In my personal experience this is one of the most impressive ways to begin a speech. Just imagine you are sitting in the audience and the man or the woman on the stage guesses exactly what you were just thinking about. Surely you would be impressed.

> *I am very sure that you have already asked yourself when the boring birthday speech will begin. There isn't such a boring speech. I have quite another idea...*

Additionally it shows that you have prepared yourself. You have tried to get into the mindset of your audience and therefore you will gain appreciation. At a rhetoric seminar for school directors I once began like this:

> *Before we begin I can promise you one thing: you won't watch any PowerPoint presentation and you don't have to fix coloured sheets of papers to a corkboard.*

For this I got thundering applause. Even if the event begins late if the air conditioning is broken or if the Christmas or thanksgiving decoration is still fixed to the ceiling: As soon as you have the feeling that your audience has a special thought right at the beginning or even before the whole event it is very helpful to address this at thought right away.

I welcomed a huge group of pupils of a well-known vocational college like this:

> *Ladies and Gentlemen, we have a problem! Not a single one of you is here voluntarily.*

That opener got a big laugh and was a wonderful ice-breaker shortly after I had begun.

50. Sentences of your target audience

Let me suggest you begin with common quotes and sentences your audience knows very well and which tell your spectators that you are a speaker on the cutting edge.

Yet again - restructuring! We are always the stupid ones. When do the managers begin their's?

You should collect these sentences in advance. Or you could listen to the traffic through the grapevine. Or you ask a few of the future participants what they expect. In preparation of my speech I have a long conversation with the host of the event every time. And each time I ask what is running through the heads of my spectators.

You may say: I know what comes next. Now he will announce the best product of all time. This year we are turning everything around...

The more correctly you hit the point the others may have said or thought, the more impressive the effect is.

Such a beginning has yet another advantage. Even if you are not a talented actor, it will be quite easy to repeat such a sentence with the right undercurrent. Even for the unexperienced speaker direct speech is easy as pie to imitate.

51. Biggest problem of your audience

The reasons for speeches are very different. But very often a common problem exists. Waiting for a new product, a beloved person has died or the audience has a concrete request. This request may be very banal.

To be upfront with it, I will be right on time with my speech. Exactly at 4.30 pm I will close my speech and you can start your weekend.

As long as the thoughts of your audience are circling around something different, they aren't really paying attention. First speak about the things by which your audience is moved.

> *You have fear! Fear that your real estate will be worthless tomorrow!*

If you put the biggest problem of your audience at the end of your speech, then you have to at least announce it.

> *I will not leave this room without having presented a solution you think doesn't exist.*

Otherwise you have to face a lack of concentration during your speech.

52. Emphasize commonalities

From sales psychology we know that similarities with the customer increase the number of sales distinctly. In regard to speeches, emphasizing similarities is among the best ideas for a good beginning.

> *Even for me our sales figures are difficult to handle. Don't believe that it is easy at the moment to keep your head straight when you are invited to a board meeting.*

If you are honest, clear and direct, the probability is high that you hit the mental state of your participants.

> *I think it was a really great lunch. Especially that chocolate cake! I couldn't resist it - a couple of times... And now would be the perfect time for a short nap, right?*

But the similarities have to exist in reality. To curry favor is not a way to raise awareness.

Don't state that everyone enjoyed himself extraordinarily when you don't have the concrete signs. This provokes the audience to think and say the opposite. It is enough to say what your personal feelings are. You enjoyed yourself, you liked it very much. Now everybody is asking themselves about their own feelings and likely the majority will agree with you.

Event oriented beginnings

Is a beginning which correlates to the content automatically an event-oriented beginning? Not necessarily. Maybe different speakers enter the stage or they were invited without them having seen a schedule or something similar. This has to be explained at the beginning, but it has to be short and right to the point.

53. Explain the occasion

When the father of the bride holds a speech, he doesn't have to tell you why. At a yoga event the European yoga-experts calls for everyone's attention. You know why. But often the audience can't build a connection at first glance matching this event and to exactly this speaker.

> *Does the brother of the bride have to say something, too? No, he doesn't. But he wants to. He likes to speak. Because he has something to say.*

> *Many of you think we are celebrating my birthday today, but...*

In a company at a big meeting it could sound like this.

> *Originally, we wanted to celebrate without any speeches today . But now I have to break this promise. I have to say something; I have to get something off my chest...*

54. Something technical

The best way to explain technical details that are important for the participants is to do so using another medium. A flipchart for example, a slide, a poster or an MC. If this isn't possible, then you have to turn this weakness into strength.

Does everyone have their mobile? Maybe you want to tweet after the session about how amazing it was. By the way, remember to switch it on again after our meeting. I am sure it's already turned off.

Sometimes it is necessary to explain a few things, before the event starts.

It's not useful to look into your handouts. There are no slides to read in my session. I am not even quite sure what I'm gonna tell you today. Because I have a different approach...

I don't have my notes on this card. This is just a prop...

Or maybe you make a joke. The speaker Derek Arden began his speech at the annual meeting of the British speaker association with

In case of a fire alarm, please leave the room first and then tweet!

In any case there is an advantage in explaining all the details before you start: You won't be interrupted during your speech.

On the other hand, there are lots of events where endless details have to be announced. Don't make the mistake of beginning your speech with: Before we begin... The beginning is the beginning.

55. Connect to the title

A birthday party or a Christmas party doesn't normally have a title. But all other events do. When I prepare for an event I spend a lot of time with the host to find a title for my speech that makes the audience curious and fits to the motto of the meeting. For the client the speech should be completely customized.

After the teaching world and the learning world now comes the communication world.

A possible challenge is to integrate the content of a speech under a special title.

Your company was built from two parts. With their own cultures, their own structures and their own strategy. Now it is important how you stay in contact with each other. If we now say "change 3.0" we mean…

Often the title is provocative or it just sounds good. And it needs a little bit of explanation to say what the subject of your speech really is.

What does communication have to do with the selling of wooden floors? Nothing at first glance…

In case of trouble it is better to have none.

I began an executive meeting under the title „take off" with presenting myself as the head of the flight crew.

A warm welcome, I'm Michael. I will be your purser for this flight 2016 into the future. Please stow away all your bad thoughts in the overhead compartments or under the seat in front of you…

Don't mention the title of your speech if we can see it on the slide behind you. We are all able to read.

!

56. Link to the previous speaker

At a big meeting for secretaries I watched Christine Weiner who spoke before me. She held a wonderful speech about the different types of bosses and she gave them names of animals. After her I began along the lines of…

Ladies, do you know what the problem is? You're not the only ones who divide your bosses into different types of character. Your bosses do it, too. There is the chipmunk secretary, the gorilla in the hallway, the office fox…

The first ten minutes I developed my speech from the speech of Christine Weiner. This was authentic, my speech benefitted from her brilliance and I couldn't have prepared this beginning.

> *If the previous speaker had spoken after me I surely would have said: Thank god that they have spoken before me. But she has spoken before me and things have become more difficult for me. How do I find a transition from the delightful world of entertainment to the deep dark recesses of human communication?*

have very rarely held a speech where I didn't mention my MC or the host or the previous speaker with at least one sentence, as long as they were nice to me. I note their name on a small cue card during their speech so that I don't forget them.

On an event for female leaders in Switzerland, the spokeswoman before me spoke about men thinking about sex for a certain amount of time during any lecture. So I came on stage with

> *I am one of those unfortunate creatures who think about sex all of the time...*

The most impressive thing is that you couldn't have prepared this. Everything you said is part of this special day. And the audience loves it. **!**

57. Connection to the date

During parties or celebrations this is easy, as well as at annual meetings which have a tradition and take place regularly over a long period of time.

The first event in a sequence, too, lends itself to being talked about at the beginning to address the special meaning of this very day.

> *Today this is an attempt, a beginning, an initiative...*

For a father, today maybe the most important day in his life.

Or the day of the speech is important because this speaker is on stage today. Maybe there will be something different in the future, maybe today is a very special day in the history of this organization.

There have never been so many people in this room as today...

If you decide today to begin something totally new, then you can...

Maybe you will ask your audience to do something differently in their lives from now on. And then today can be a very important day in retrospect.

On the day of a big speech you always read the newspaper, watch the morning news and spend a few minutes on the internet. You don't want to mention a problem that was solved or got worse last night. Or the role-model you give died early this morning or was handcuffed and taken to court. Don't laugh, this has all happened already. **!**

58. Last year

An exception is the first event in a series of events. There the only issue is to talk about the fact that this event didn't exist last year at this time and why this event probably will take place next year.

Otherwise, there is always a before, a pre-conference last month, year, decade. You can always remind us of this fact and build a connection.

I can't believe that the year is already over. The place is different, but although so many things have happened in the world...

*When I stood here last year I felt quite different. I was
under lots of pressure and I had no experience how to cope
with...*

Sometime it can be helpful to remind someone of something bad,
so that it never will happen again. But naturally it is much easier
when your memories are good memories.

*I just have to say three words: Bowling, basement and
Champagne. And everybody who is laughing now was
there. For all the others it could be worthwhile to ask
someone later this evening what happened there last year...*

It is not necessary to explain at length how time has gone by and
how quickly we are getting older. But to evoke good emotions is
a good preparation for the content of your speech. Every smile
about the past now belongs to you. You were the trigger or the
activator for the positive emotion.

Activating beginnings

59. Ask for a show of hands

Unlike rhetorical questions, real questions to the whole audience are always a good opportunity for a thrilling beginning. You could really ask your participants something. The only thing is that you need the answer for your speech.

Who thinks that this meeting should have taken place last year?

Who now expects us to talk about sales?

Who believes that answer A is right?

It would be most elegant if the result of the show of hands is not right. Then everybody would be wide awake.

The American professor of psychology Daniel Gilbert and some others have the audience take a lot of decisions during their speeches.

Are there more dogs or more pigs in Oxford?

Where is the child mortality higher, in...?

Will the population of the world increase, decrease or stay the same over the next 100 years?

Then they show us that many of our assumptions are totally wrong or based on wrong preconditions. And then they explain why. A beginning like this is very inspiring, because no one likes to make mistakes.

Please, don't ask questions whether someone wants to be happier in the future or who has already been in a difficult situation. That gets on everybody's nerves. Or if you, for example, don't do anything, with the answer following the question: "Who has children?" the audience becomes **!**

ingry. Especially those participants who have listened to such a speech before will become irritable.

60. Ask for an answer

A variation of the show of hands is to ask a question of estimation. Ask your audience to a random number which proofs something for or against your thesis, you will soon postulate.

What do you think? How many percent...

How many people are here today?

Everybody will think about the answer and your audience is activated from the first moment on. But you can change every scientific result into an estimation question for all your listeners.

61. A question to the audience

It is not necessary that it happens with scientific rules. Before your speech you can ask for opinions, you can ask spectators and you can send emails to peers or employees.

I just walked around. What do you think...

How many answers did I get to my email? What is your opinion?

If the event or the seat-arrangement allows, you can ask a few people at the beginning.

Why are you here today?

How many times have you been here?

You can ask for a mood feedback. It is a perfect way to pick up your audience. The likelihood that the other listeners will find themselves represented by the answers is high.

62. A play with numbers

It is easier said than done to invent a play with numbers. But in the 21.century we can find anything on the internet. And you can put any number in a surprising context to make it more understandable.

Do you know that there are as many chickens on earth as people?

If you took a part of the sun as large as a pinhead, this tiny piece would burn everything in a 70 mile radius.

99 percent of all kinds of life, which have lived on earth, are extinct.

In a hand full of soil there are more beings than people on earth.

I could go on and on now for hours. But you can also develop such play of numbers by yourself.

If our birthday boy had received a coin for every moment he helped someone else, he would...

Imagine only one percent of your products would last 3 years longer...

Such plays of numbers are simply invented and can be very astonishing for people who are not so familiar with the subject.

63. An exercise

It would be a very surprising beginning, to start simply with an exercise. Let the audience do something at the beginning, let them test something. Give them a little experiment. The mentalist and speaker Thorsten Havener sometimes immediately begins his speech with a little request.

Please interlace your fingers. Which thumb is on the top?
And now please switch thumbs. Not very comfortable, is it?

This is the wrong beginning to a ceremonial event. But in many cases the speech could begin with a little exercise for the audience. Even if it is only imaginary.

Close your eyes. Imagine you are sitting on the beach. A light wind...

Please concentrate on the spiral on my slide...

Professional speakers are systematically looking for exercises and other possibilities to bring the audience into action. Change is especially welcomed during long events. Why not begin like this?

Use only short and very simple exercises at the beginning. The spectators don't trust you yet. Normally, you as the speaker have to deliver something, before the audience is willing to stand up or possibly to touch their neighbors. If everyone is totally overwhelmed by your performance, you can get people to do anything. But again don't put any softener phrases in the question to your audience: "I would like that you possibly may stand up and I would be very much appreciated if someone maybe now...

!

Dramatic beginnings

64. A conundrum

Conundrum is a big word. What I mean is something to which your audience has no answer to. Not even you need to have an answer. It only should inspire your audience to think and to get access to your subject. The audience should be activated.

Can you tell me what's going on in people's head when they're standing at a completely empty intersection at midnight, no car in sight waiting for the traffic light to turn green?

It can also be a real puzzle, of course. Or a very personal one.

Gerhard, at the age of 17, had to fill in a questionnaire in the school magazine, because he wanted to become a student speaker. What do you think it read under "career choice"?

Thinking, pondering, answering questions... perfect possibilities to win an audience immediately.

It is black, round and has never been seen in your company before.

What do you think? How many of our televisions in polystyrene packaging fit on a truck?

We all love quiz shows where we can guess. Take advantage of this fact.

65. Humor

Telling a joke is not always a good beginning, as you may have guessed already. Maybe the joke was simply too bad? Regardless whether it was a joke or a humorous anecdote, when people had a heartfelt laugh at the beginning, it wasn't the worst start.

With the help of the Internet, you can find numerous punchlines that are even sorted by topic. It's easy to find something suitable. But it really becomes exciting when you rewrite punchlines, tailoring them to the target group.

Surgery is the art of cutting away so many organs from a person that he or she is able to pay the surgeon.

You can rewrite this joke pattern for other professional groups. And one thing I'm sure you won't hear: the phrase "I already knew it!" My experience has shown me that spectators like to laugh, even if the punch line may not be new.

What's the difference between a hill and a pill? A hill is hard to get up, a pill is hard to get down.

To invent jokes and punchlines, you can best use existing joke formulas that are already known to your audience. "What's-the-difference-jokes" are easy to invent. You take a term from the area you are going to talk about and make an unusual reference.

What is the difference between a speaker and an emergency? None. Both occur and spread terror.

Let's think of something that fits the theme.

What is the difference between you and your colleagues at Siemens?

There are climax jokes.

The climax of topicality is when the speaker does not even know what he is talking about.

Negation offers many possibilities

We'll never know what we don't want if we don't do what we can't do.

Needless to say, no one could ever be not disturbed by no sense of humor.

The good and the bad message is another pattern.

The good message is that I will be finished in five minutes...

The last words formula joke...

The last words of a bad speaker? – Only 60 slides left.

Jokes with a paradox.

Paradox is when some of you appear numerous.

Abbreviations are easy to find, or syndromes.

We all suffer from the NIB-Syndrome: No one Is Better.

Or light bulb jokes

How many of you do we need to screw in a light bulb...

And if you have an enumeration on your subject, make sure that the third word of the enumeration is funny.

It's easy to quit smoking. All you need is strong will, determination and wet matches.

But also exaggerations, talking animals, crucifixion jokes, cannibal jokes, Mr. Top Jokes, bad definitions, optimist pessimist jokes or simple one-liners are quickly invented.

66. Contradiction

Since Paul Watzlawick's book "How to fail most successfully" or Tucholsky's "Tips for a bad speaker", the idea of getting attention by wishing, expecting or demanding the opposite of what one actually wants has become envogue.

Do me one favour. Please leave your phones on. I am a big fan of fancy ringtones. If you want to leave the room and come in again and get out, just do it. I have learned that I have to activate the audience. And for God's sake, don't ask questions, it freaks me out.

The audience will listen again, because it is different to what they normally hear at the beginning of an event.

Let's make it very short. Don't get in a good mood. And most important, don't drink anything. The best thing to do would be to not talk to anyone at all.

From my perspective you don't have to reveal that.

You've already guessed that this was a joke.

The audience does understand this without an explanation. But most of the speakers lose their courage and they have the feeling that they must explain how it was meant.

67. Do something

Simple and effective. Tear something! Throw something! Fold something! If you know how to, juggle, balance, play catch, make a knot, play an instrument or make an artistic exercise... Do it!

For example like this: A box under every arm, a package between your legs and one under your chin. The speaker tries to enter the stage like this. And then he builds a connection to the swamped employees.

Or you paint a steep upward curve with your hand in the air, flatten the curve and say?

And now?

The speaker Peter Zinn shows us a little tennis ball (logics) and a huge gymnastic ball (emotions) and asks:

If they fight, who do you think's gonna win?

The audience won't forget the picture so quickly. However, it is best if you work without props or use what you find on site at the event or what you know is available for sure.

Perhaps like this: The speaker pours two thirds of a bottle into a large bucket. Then he turns the bottle over and says:

For most of us, the better half of our lives is already over.

The speaker and bestselling author Lothar Seiwert uses a folding rule, which he breaks apart on the same subject step by step into smaller and smaller pieces.

Of course, large props cases are also allowed, but there really has to be a good gag. After all, your spectators will see you moving back to the station with your wardrobe trunk.

68. Build tension

In prepared speeches, as most are, you can stage the suspense a in a good "crime scene". After all, the audience loves tension.

Imagine if there was a sentence where no woman could say "no". Would you be interested? Even if you don't believe it. There is this sentence. And you will get to know it today.

At the end of your presentation, the audience will automatically remind you to come back to this point. With this introduction and the resolution, the speaker Stefan Spies always creates wonderful arc of tension at the end. Every Oscar award ceremony works according to this principle.

The winners have been chosen. The names are right here in this envelope. Irrevocably. They can no longer be influenced. And it was a very exciting race.

Even though in many books I preach that you should immediately present the most important thing in lectures, the exception again confirms the rule. Sometimes torture is the right way for th audience to keep the tension. But then you have to announce that something exciting or special is about to come.

That was the greatest insight I have gained in recent years...

Now you can begin at the beginning.

69. Personalize objects

This isn't something for every purpose. But how about letting the camera you want to present speak for itself as a living creature? What would it say? How would it like the event? Which kind of feelings could it have?

Wow, I was really excited today! Finally, I will tell you what is so special about me.

An interview with the hiking boots of the birthday boy or girl or with the door knob in the finance department can create a very good beginning.

If our meeting room could talk, what would it say?

How does the audience know that the objects are speaking? Quite easy. Talk to it. We will know very well what is meant.

Hello, new package? How are you doing?

It can be very effective to personalize abstract things. Let's talk with the future, rant with the team spirit or you enter the stage as...

It doesn't matter whether you play a role of a puppy or an object or the talking fear – don't change your voice or adjust it. Give your artificial figure another posture (nervous, relaxed, excited), and its voice can be distinguished at once from yours. However if you want to change your voice, take care that you don't make an effort of it. If you stress your voice because you are playing

!

81

Cinderella with a squeaky voice or the dangerous wolf with a very low voice then you also stress the audience. Some CDs for children are hard to listen to.

Courageous beginnings

70. Praise yourself

Some speakers don't even have to be told that. They do this on their own and tell anyone who doesn't want to know how great they are and list their great successes. Everyone else can think about whether it wouldn't be a good start to spread a little complacency.

Can you understand my pride? Can you understand that I am very pleased with the decisions I made last year? It was a joint achievement, but I am very relieved that last autumn I let nobody change my mind about the new strategy.

And if you exaggerate a little, everybody listens to you because it's unusual and because there might be something to laugh about.

The trouble is, I won't fit into a suit anymore. My ID is wrong now. I've grown 20 centimeters since last Tuesday.

I will spare you the warning to only use this type of beginning rarely and very cautiously. But there are also many people who make themselves as though they were not important. Even if many things have depended on them in the past months and the success is for the most part their merit.

71. Talking about yourself in the 3rd person

Let's say something didn't go so well in the past. And let's say you were the cause. Then you can apologize. However, it may also be easier to speak of oneself in the third person.

This person is ashamed today. He's angry and would like to undo everything. And that person is me.

It certainly requires a little rethinking to approach a topic like this.

This Michael Rossié is a strange guy. He says something totally different about rhetoric and communication than what I have learned.

But you also have completely new possibilities.

Sometimes he makes me so angry with his "We have to make it!" That always sounds so lordly and arrogant. He may not even mean it, but it comes across that way.

Imagine you had similar thoughts about the speaker. Wouldn't it be amusing if the speaker on stage expressed these very thoughts? Wouldn't that make you very, very close to him?

At a birthday party I gave a lecture to a friend about the negative side of her character (last name), she should take an example from the positive side of her character (first name).

72. A provocation

Not that I'm a big fan of provocation, but myriads of success coaches and top speakers like to do this. And they are certainly among the speakers who will win over their audience the most and earn the highest fees.

Yes, ladies and gentlemen, all around you are winners and champignons. How does it feel to be the loser in the big game of life?

Maybe not very likeable, but even I do that from time to time. Today, the internet provides you with much more information about your viewers than some people would like. Let's assume that your audience is numerically manageable and it's about online communication.

I was just looking at your internet pages for a while. Only one was so good that we should even mention it.

A well-placed provocation at the beginning ensures you one hundred percent attention in any case. If you feel a headwind in the audience, it is undoubtedly better than no emotion at all.

Marketing guru Scott Stratten began his keynote speech at the National Speakers Association Convention with the sentence:

Hello, room full of competitors, how are you?

And in some cases the provocation also serves very well to elegantly invalidate the resulting requests. Between you and me: This can be really fun, because you know exactly what's coming and are well prepared.

The mentor and speaker Thomas Göller called his workshop at a speaker meeting:

Why does my competitor (such a deadbeat) make so much money and I don't?"

Before I get bored with the seven golden rules for a goal-oriented conversation, I prefer to go to such a workshop. The provocation leads to increased attention.

73. Fox the audience

I have to open a VIP lounge in a hotel and of course I have to give everyone the boring information that management and architect imagined, from the choice of materials to the invested capital.

At the same time it should be entertaining. So I'll start with a typical presenter's chant.

Ladies and gentlemen. Let us use the next hour to familiarize ourselves a little with the architectonic concept. For this purpose, a small recourse to the history of art is absolutely necessary...

Then I interrupt quite abruptly.

Did you get scared now? No, we're not going on like this.

And then I told what I wasn't going to talk about and of course I did it. I fooled my audience for a moment. And the relief that followed was a nice start.

Just one second. I'll be gone in a minute. Mrs. Substitute will represent me, because I have a more important appointment today...

Don Yaeger began his speech with

Hello... umh....Phoenix!

The Speaker Nigel Risner is a master of foxing the audience. He began with

I have two presentations with me. One about rhetoric, one about my wife and our two children. Which one do you want?

He shows the audience a slide with the words OPPORTUNITY IS NOWHERE. After a few seconds he changes the spaces OPPORTUNITY IS NOW HERE.

The speaker Dave Newman began his workshop

17 tips on how to become happier and more successful. - That was just the title to get you into the workshop. 17 points always sounds good.

Thomas Skipwith enters the stage with a very large triangular Toblerone bar and says:

Square! Practical! Good!

This is a slogan from one of Toblerone's biggest competitors. That's the way to go!

I was once hired to give a cabaret farewell speech for a bank executive. I ordered a guard's uniform from that bank and burst very loudly into the middle of the celebration.

Please, pack up all things and leave the room as soon as possible. There's nothing to celebrate here today. Tomorrow Mr. Leavenow will be here and until then a lot of things have to be prepared.

Then I told them what was going to happen tomorrow and chatted about the member of the board who was sitting right in front of me the whole time. Afterwards I was terrified because I was obviously wrong in the day.

Many, many years ago, one of the most beautiful cabaret evenings of my life was called "Lore Lorentz und die Pürkels" in the "Kommödchen" in Dusseldorf. The curtain rises and the stage is full of props from a group of artists that Lore Lorentz is now moderating.

But the Pürkels aren't here yet. So Lore Lorenz says something to fill the gap, begins again with the warm-up, checks where they re, bridges again..... You can guess the punch line: Throughout the program, the Pürkels do not appear at all. Only the entire equipment for an artist troop stands unused on stage, while Lore Lorentz moves like a foreign body within it. It's a wonderful turn to tie me up. Because they may still be coming.

74. Frighten the audience

Before you write me letters: don't drive your audience away, of course. But a fright that dissolves into relief is an excellent way of keeping all eyes on yourself. We just saw that when I told you about fooling the audience.

I'm sorry, but the person sitting next to you is a fraud.

Now you can expand on that a little and then explain that there is desire to cheat in all of us. One more, the other less.

I will not bore you with a long speech. I can also do it with a short one.

87

It will only take three hours. But these three, maximum four hours will change your life in the long run!

No matter what happens now. After such a strange beginning will listen better now. Maybe it's exciting. Anything that triggers an emotion increases attention, even if the emotion turns out to be a false alarm. Now the audience is wide awake.

Karaoke was announced after the break at a big event of several banks and insurance companies on Lake Zurich in Switzerland.

Take a look under your seat. Those of you, who have a piece of paper under your seat, please come forward to sing karaoke here...

There were indeed many spectators with notes under their chairs but of course there was no Karaoke afterwards. The relief about that was huge, first for those who didn't have a note and then for those who didn't have to sing. A loud murmur - the midday low had been overcome.

But also a bang is conceivable, a hasty movement or a flash of light. A fright that turns out to be harmless awakens. Even a troublemaker who turns out to be an accomplice can make for a very surprising start.

75. Ignore the audience

Imagine you enter the stage and pretend that the hall is completely empty. Now you are talking to yourself and we learn what will happen or would happen if someone was there.

If they come in right now, I'll pretend that nothing special is going on. Then I will put on a very meaningful face...

It takes a bit of acting skill to ignore an audience that is there. That's why you should rehearse it. You have to think carefully about what you are doing while you are talking to yourself: Set up the projector, set up the documents, walk off the stage.

would definitely be a start that everyone will remember for months to come.

> *It's the wrong room. I am sure of that. You don't miss Hermann's birthday party after all. Nobody misses it. And I have prepared such a great speech. And now there is nobody here...*

The art is to get it done in such a way that everyone gets the impression that you are speaking to yourself. You allow the viewers a glimpse into your world of thoughts and can thus convey completely different information than with a classic speech. It's a bit like an off-text in a movie.

76. The audience begins

At a conference in America I saw Jeff Jarvis. He is the author of "What would google do?" And if you like, he didn't even start it. He didn't give a speech at all. He let the swarm intelligence speak. He went straight to the audience and started to network the knowledge of the audience with each other. This "speech" will also remain in my memory for a long time.

It is possible that in the near future there will be fewer and fewer people passing on knowledge from the stage to the audience, but knowledge will be exchanged among the audience itself. But you could start with a question, what are we supposed to do now?

> *I am not holding a speech now. I thought you might say something. We want to talk about your problems today. It does not make sense for the boss to say anything. I mean that seriously. I am not saying anything from now on...*

You could ask the audience to say a sentence about the new project or about the person who has a birthday. Or you can ask them to call out statements into the room that have been annoying them for days.

Now you can still let your thoughts flow in. Or they can talk about why so few or so many people come forward.

The few reflections show me that we are doing something fundamentally wrong...

Here, the speaker becomes more of a moderator, of a facilitator of an initiator. And that doesn't mean that we have less of an outcome.

Formats like the Bar Camp or the Un-Conference can be very exciting and instructive. But it takes a lot of courage to get involved with such formats and a bit of experience to work with them.

77. Be quiet

A popular exercise at an acting school is to enter the stage, open your mouth, and then say nothing. Then the time was stopped who makes it the longest time without boring the audience. Several failed attempts, then the courage leaves the speaker or he wants to start differently. Or he despairs because he can't do it. The cabaret artist Gerhard Polt once managed to remain silent on stage for seven minutes before the show started.

Speaker Slatco Sterzenbach does nothing for a whole minute at the beginning of his lecture to show how many thoughts we have in this time.

A much simpler option is to talk about the fact that you won't talk about it. Because it is unnecessary, because everything has already been said, because the new product speaks for itself, because you get angry.

I am not going to say anything about this now. You can wait as long as you want. I cannot stand that, you think? But I can stand that. I will prove that to you. I say nothing, nothing at all. I am not even saying that...

At a vernissage I once introduced an artist. But I kept telling the audience that I wasn't telling them that the artist was from Hamburg, because it wasn't anyone's business. And so I gradually got rid of all the information, the supposedly important ones and the supposedly unimportant ones. At least an unusual beginning.

Beginnings for actors

78. Role plays

You could go on stage in a certain role. Speaker Michael Ehlers appears as Dr. Hein Hansen, a pretty real copy of a Hamburg fish seller.

But I've also seen managers as James Bond or as Tyra Banks who unfortunately doesn't have a picture with her today.

You can appear as a racing reporter.

I'm reporting here live from the birthday party of Markus. The guests have arrived, the first speakers have just been announced...

I have also given lectures as a caricature of a speaker, or as an insecure beginner. The magician and speaker Gaston Florin enters the stage as a nervous, extremely bad speaker and shows through the slow change of body language how to radiate security, witty and memorable.

The speaker as nurse for the sick company...

A teacher who distributes school grades

A fairy godmother

The salesman at a funfair

The presenter Michael Sporer once staged the meeting of a big company as a television show without a camera being seen far and wide. He acted as if there were different shots, as if he was getting instructions from a director and had the audience do everything that you would let a real audience do, if it was really recorded. It must have been a very funny evening for everyone.

79. A scene or a dialog

You don't have to be an actor to play a scene. Ultimately, it's all about letting two or three people speak. Literal speech is often the most authentic and lively part of speeches and lectures and a good seasoning for any speech. That's how I started my lecture at the Stuttgart Knowledge Forum:

> *Two speakers meet. One says to the other: "Are you in Stuttgart this year?" The other one answers: "Yes! And both know exactly what they are talking about. They are talking about today. I am very proud to be a part of this event.*

Such a beginning is very simple. Everyone knows that there has never been such a dialogue, but the message is clear. A real dialogue is also a good introduction to a speech. The fact that you heard it is easy to stage.

> *I remember the day when Peter stormed into my office and said, "I found her!" - What did you find? I asked. And he lights up at me and says: "The woman of my life!*

> *"Is the boss really going through with this to the end?" - Yes, he is pulling it through! - "Wanna bet that he won't do it?" - Ladies and gentlemen, you would have lost the bet.*

Every dialogue tells the truth between the lines. And the listeners are immediately in the middle of a scene. It couldn't be more exciting.

80. Sing

Now, don't say you can't sing. It's about singing a few bars. Instead of speaking of the familiar song what a wonderful world, you can simply sing the first line. This is much easier than it looks. Suitable are also

> *We are the champions...*

Do it baby one more time...

We all live in a yellow submarine...

Money, money, money

Tonight's the night...

Another one bites the dust!

That can sound a bit crooked. But with most songs you don't just transport a line, but also a rhythm, a feeling, a mood, and that can be very helpful at the beginning. And if you can't sing at all, just speak the first line like text.

81. Produce noise with a microphone

There are specialists, for example in a cappella groups, who are able to get the most wonderful things out of a microphone. You are completely amazed at how you can change a tone and what is possible with two lips and a tongue.

If you call on the help of a technician, the number of possibilities increases many times over. Of course, this is much easier with a handheld microphone than with a clip-on microphone or a headset. This is why many well-known speakers swear on using a microphone that they can pick up.

Take a microphone, put your hand around the head of the microphone and, in combination with a nasal voice, the wonderful copy of an airplane captain or a train attendant at the Deutsche Bahn is created.

You can imitate machines, suggest rhythms, use sighs and deep inhalers. You can whisper and grind your teeth, you can simulate colds, speech or language mistakes and imitate throaty or breathy-sounding voices.

Even with a very small sound generator, which is actually too quiet for a large room, you can achieve great effects with the microphone. For example, with music boxes, bells, musical instruments or children's toys. Creativity is also required here.

82. Parody

You don't have to be a great actor to do a parody. When in a group that knows each other well, I ask everyone to parody each other, sometimes a single movement, a single sentence, a single reaction is enough to recognize the other person immediately. It's quick and easy.

Just one thing... (Peter Falk in „Inspector Columbo")

Dumbass (Red Forman in that 70 show)

I am ready (sponge bob)

But even people whom everyone knows are suitable for a parody. Play a David Letterman copy that introduces a real guest to the saturday night live show.

If you start well with "You are here because you are worth it" or I'm lovin it" or if you make the peace or the victory sign, everyone knows what or who is meant now.

Why not imitate colleagues, employees or bosses? Why not poke fun at team meetings or look at your discussion round in a funny way or look at e-mails and circulars from a new perspective by making a few small changes or adjustments.

If you do that lovingly and your viewers say: *"That's exactly the way it is!"* you've already half won. The exaggeration has made it clear.

Gerriet Danz has written a wonderful book in which he exaggerates PowerPoint presentations in such a way that you are deliciously amused.

Opening Christmas presents with PowerPoint.

A marriage proposal with PowerPoint.

The 10 commandments as a presentation.

Very funny, very instructive and at the same time it made me very thoughtful.

83. Make a telephone call

For example, play the call when you were invited to the event that was taking place. Maybe it was funny, surprising, interesting. But you need to think about it a little before you go. Simply repeating what was said at the other end is the worst of all possibilities when simulating a telephone conversation alone.

How should it be? Of course it is humorous! Eh clear: Nothing against the competition. Yes, and not too difficult. After all, it's the big annual meeting. I already know.

The easiest way is, of course, when the telephone conversation was like this:

Wouldn't you like to perform something at the company party? But I do understand. If you have so much to do... And your wife? I have already called Gerda. She can't either. She is having problems with her vocal cords...

In a short time you can play a series of telephone conversation in which we do not understand what you are trying to achieve. You will then explain this to us when you have "dropped out of the role".

You don't need to bring a phone or use your mobile phone for such simple scenes. One hand as a handset is all you need. And most professionals don't take them either. After the first "Hello, who am I talking to?" everyone has understood that we are on the phone. And if I let two people talk, a small change of posture is enough to make the audience understand that someone else is talking now.

84. Performe a mime

Especially if you are not a professional, a mime can be a surprising beginning. It is not about creating spaces or landscapes in the imagination of the audience. It's more about the silent scene at the beginning, which shows what you want to achieve with your speech.

Demonstrate how to use the new product or the new object that everyone is familiar with.

Wait impatiently to show that most meetings in the company start unpunctually.

Pluck around pretty long to show that everything has to be perfect.

Once you get involved with an object, whether you're trying on hats, testing imaginary weapons, or fighting the malice of the object, once you know exactly what you can do on stage, playing a mime becomes easier. Even if a real mime would do that with an imaginary object, you can still pick something up concrete.

Allow your viewers to watch you get your pay slip, read an email from the boss, enter the company in the morning or try to work without being disturbed.

Slides in the background can help explain where we are. The same applies to music, noises or recorded sentences and quotes from other people. But that puts us at a beginning with technology. That always becomes a bit more elaborate.

Technical beginnings

85. A photo

An extraordinary photo, a funny snapshot or a touching photomontage can be a wonderful entry. You'll certainly find that on the Internet, but your own photo is always better and, more importantly, you have the rights.

86. A film

It is no longer a problem to show films in between form a technical standpoint. If you are sure that the film was not "clicked on" by everyone on Facebook last week, this is an excellent way to undivided attention.

Interviews, cartoons, trailers etc. are very impressive as an introduction. However, you still have the same problem with the rights as with the photos. If possible, make your own film!

87. Music

Music can be background music, but also introduction and prelude. Many well-known speakers come on stage with special music. Make sure that the type of music creates the mood, the lyrics of a song are of secondary importance.

Once upon a time in the west...

The Sting...

I like to move it, move it...

Particularly distant places can be created with music very well for all.

Oriental sounds...

Country and Western music

ust a few bars are enough and the music conveys much more tmosphere than any long manual could ever convey.

And if you should actually play an instrument, then you can not only underlay singing, but also your speech with tones and hythms.

88. A caricature

A drawn joke, a caricature of a person or a symbolic scene for lealing with one another. A good cartoonist can give you an ffective message for your foil or flip chart with just a few trokes.

And if you don't have any other slides, this symbol can remain isible throughout the presentation and thus form the basis for vhat you want to say to the audience.

89. A scrolling text

n the cinema the credits are shown after the film. Filmmakers ome up with a lot of ideas to make it read. After all, many people vere involved in the film. A text that runs through the picture, hat is possibly animated, a hand that writes some thoughts on an maginary screen.

t's easy to create something like this for the beginning of a peech and it creates a surprising effect.

90. Draw something

A good opener can be a funny drawing on a flipchart or an xpressive lettering. Imagine you calmly enter the stage, go to he flip chart and slowly start drawing. All the attention is now vith you.

On modern tablet PCs you can also paint around to your heart's content in PowerPoint presentations. I saw this for the first time with Klaus J. Fink, and it was very effective. Change a drawing, add something to a slide. Erase it. In any case, it's an unusual beginning.

From the visualization coach Johannes Sauer I learned how easy it is to stick other drawn objects or figures into existing drawings on the flipchart and take them out again or to remove previously prepared stickers and thus achieve great effects. Such a flipchart sheet can be used more often.

91. A clock starts ticking

Time is precious. Your time is limited. A ticking watch is a very effective way to point out how you want to deal with this time.

And if you then pick up the symbol again at the end and the time reaches 00:00, this can be associated with almost any message. Especially under time pressure.

92. A slideshow

For longer events you can start with a few photos from yesterday evening. You can show the new product on beautiful photos from all sides, without saying anything or you can fade in pictures with the company goals for the next year.

The speaker and rhetoric trainer Andreas Bornhäußer welcomes every participant on a slide at the beginning of the seminar. These slides run in an endless loop during the waiting time. That really impressed me. And even more of course the participants, whose names were written correctly.

I once coached a speaker who only had 10 minutes to present a charity project at an event. I gave her the tip to ask the organizer if they could already present photos of the project as an endless loop on the screen when the audience entered the room. That was possible in this case, and both gained from it: For the audience there is something to watch while waiting, the project becomes more present and the speaker saved time during his speech.

93. Video greeting

Whether the international boss, the local district administrator or a celebrity: If there's someone you can connect to, the better. And if he also announces you via video, it increases your market value. Such videos are easy and inexpensive to produce today. A small film, taken with a smartphone on a telescope holder, is enough.

94. A collage of sounds

We are already close to the next section with the complex beginnings. But imagine that noises, shreds of conversation, sounds and signals are coming from all sides of the room.

Possibly there are even loudspeakers fastened under the seats. The illusion of being somewhere in the middle of all these sounds could leave a very strong impression: on a horse racecourse, in the crowded subway, on a construction site or in a kindergarten.

But of course it's also possible with less effort. Imagine you come on stage and you hear a busy sound on a telephone.

Beep, beep, beep…

Or a mixture of mobile ringtones, or murmuring or a bleating flock of sheep or shattering glass or shots…

95. Use a prop

It is not necessary to show a model of our brain to explain where our thoughts come from. But a picture is often not as impressive as the object itself.

Dribble with a ball on stage.

Drag a ladder with you!

Set up a folding chair!

Hold the prototype of the new product in your hand.

I trained the members of the board to go public, without the executives having a single product of their company physically with them.

But also props which stand for something like a whip, a lunchbox or a pair of sport shoes could create a very good beginning.

The speaker Lutz Langhoff spends large parts of his lectures on a really high unicycle, which he can only get on with the help of others. You won't forget it.

Or the speaker Johannes Warth. He shoots candles with arrows. And if you are now saying that this is not possible in your room - Johannes Warth would pull it off.

96. An electronical survey of the audience

Today there are great technical possibilities to capture the opinion of the audience directly. At a large publishing house everyone got a kind of smartphone in their hands and could choose between four alternatives, which were thrown onto the wall on slides. So the speaker was in constant contact with the entire audience, who could tell him things in the vote that were not so pleasant.

A: The action was really great

B: The action was helpful

C: The action was superfluous

D: I was angry about the action

Now the audience was able to experience live how the executive board is confronted with the results of the survey and what it has to say about it. That was a real dialogue with a large group.

At a convention in America, speaker Sally Hogshead went one step further. On the day before her presentation, she pointed out a questionnaire on the internet, which we should all please fill out. And the next day she presented the results of the survey, in which one was involved, on stage. Very unusual. She spoke of no one but the group sitting in front of her, and I was one of them.

Challenging beginnings

97. A mask

Come with a mask. This is not such a big effort. That doesn't have to be the perfect latex mask. Get the picture from the Internet, cut out of paper with two holes for the eyes and a slit for the mouth and you can appear as a celebrity. Either someone who is prominent in public life or a celebrity within your company or organization.

But you can also be an Albert Einstein, an Elvis, a TV presenter or a comedian.

98. Dress yourself up

That doesn't mean you're wearing a carnival costume. But a garment that stands for the person you honour. A fan scarf of your club or casual clothes as a symbol that you don't have to worry about the future. This could also have an impressive effect.

Come as a circus director!

Stick a red nose in your face!

You can appear as a chimney sweep!

Appear as Sherlock Holmes.

Give it to the border control!

May I see your documents, please!

Come in your doctor's coat or as a typical controller. Speaker Edgar K. Geffroy has already come on stage in mountain climbing gear.

99. A puppet

You don't have to be a ventriloquist to bring a doll or a stuffed animal on stage as a conversation partner or demonstration object. And this doll could also begin and welcome you.

Perhaps you still need a table or a holder for the doll. But if you like the idea, it would be easy to organize.

But be careful! The puppet must continue to play along and defrost again and again during the rest of the lecture. Just introducing a puppet as an opening gag, which is then forgotten, usually is resented by the audience.

100.   A magic trick

If you can do something like that, it's wonderful. But you should be able to do it perfectly. Nothing worse than a magic trick where the magician has to concentrate enormously. The audience would feel sorry for him and any interest in the content of the speech would go out of the window. Trainer and speaker Gaby S. Graupner started the annual convention during her presidency by changing her dress in seconds (!) during her presentation. That was the talk of the day, but she had to practice that meticulously beforehand. You don't just do that quickly.

More beginnings

No, we are not at the end. We are just simply ending it. Not because I can't think of anything else, but because the number 100 has, unfortunately, already been reached. There are still infinitely many further possibilities.

Why not do something wrong at the beginning? Have a tongue twister, come from the wrong side! Do something that is obviously a mistake. And the relief that the mistake was only played will again provide suspense. It takes a bit of courage, but it's not difficult.

With **blacklight** you can achieve special effects. Only white garments can be seen brightly, black ones not. So heads can move without bodies or hands can be alone on the way.

Especially when a second person is involved, the number of possible effects increases significantly. What you previously thought was one person's arms and legs are suddenly two.

Implement **dancing elements**. Or you can let dancers around you perform what you're saying, a danced speech, so to speak. Take a look at John Bohannon on the internet. That's really great. Music or musical instruments can add a rhythm to your speech. This is also very effective, especially at the beginning.

It's even better if you can dance yourself. Then dance the beginning. A few tango steps or a turn on the toes will give you a good start.

Maybe you can do even more? Standing on your head? Turning a wheel, handstand overturning? The American speaker Dan Thurmon sweeps over the stage with **the greatest tricks**. And people are already waiting for the next salto in the air.

106

The speaker and presenter Bernhard Wolff can **perfectly speak backwards** and then play it right around for you. By now he can even do this singing.

When you're on a big stage, you can take advantage of the light. You are standing in a cone of light, a **stroboscope** bathes the stage in bright flashes of light, in which your performance seems to be danced and you create any mood you want with colorful light. If that works, use it.

Among actors you say "If the director doesn't know what to do, he uses **dry ice**". So if you can't think of anything else, then white fog is drifting over the stage, from which the speakers now merge like an apparition from another world. With an esoteric message this can also be effective.

And if you have helpers and if all depends on a big event that will be really good and the participants should still talk about it days later, then do a **flash mob.** Ask the audience to call in, disturb or seemingly take over the direction after a fixed dramaturgy. Your audience will be frightened, the attention is at 100 percent, and the relief that everything is a staging will clearly lift the mood. Here you have the maximum height of fall that every good moment of tension needs.

We once opened a convention of the German Speakers Association like that and everyone still remembers this years later. That's when the troublemakers started singing after the first horror. And that's what they call a **musical flash mob.**

On the Internet you will find countless examples of flash mobs. One of the most beautiful ones is by John Reynolds, who presented a social media platform. The film of it is, unfortunately, no longer online. But take a look at Colin Robertson at ted.com.

Maybe you can't be seen at all. Your voice comes from **the off** the stage remains empty. Then people gradually discover who is speaking to them as you come forward.

And if you don't like any of these proposals, you'll **rant at your audience**. Tell them what you think about them. I guarantee you Then there's really something going on!

Keep discovering, be creative. It is always unforgivable to bore a group of people. They have all come just for you, your company or because of an occasion to celebrate. And you should no disappoint them. Provide for an impressive experience.

Only those who constantly come up with something new are ahead of the competition.

Even more beginnings

That's still not enough for you? You want to develop something yourself? Then I recommend searching a beautiful old business directory. Whether the local one or the yellow pages, such a book is a treasure. It shows our whole life, at least for the next four or five years.

Pull out the register at the end of the business directory and go through it every now and then. You'll be surprised at how many wonderful suggestions you get that you would otherwise never have had. The creative muscle also needs inspiration from time to time.

My three favorite beginnings

There are three beginnings that I myself particularly like to use and often implement. Sometimes in addition to the beginning I had originally prepared.

First of all it is important for me to mention place or time (**beginning 41 or 42**) in order to give the audience a beginning that is only for them. An introduction that cannot be repeated on another evening is a form of appreciation towards the audience.

Secondly, I like to speak a few of my thoughts out loud (**beginning 43**). That's the easiest thing for me. And things have to come out simply because they remind me of something or because they are important to me. To say thank you is often part of it. Or the joy of being invited somewhere or being allowed to speak. I constantly try to keep my appreciation for the profession of a speaker over the years.

And third, I try to figure out what the audience is probably thinking right there and then (**beginning 49).** When I get that, it's the best possible start. The audience feels understood and picked up. Now it becomes much easier to guide them through a topic or issue for an hour or two.

Try out what is good for you. When you've finished reading the book you will like some ideas especially well. Exactly these are worth trying out for the first time. And regarding the pages with the beginnings making you frown you should simply tear them out!

Last preparations

You are now ready and you have prepared all the technical requirements. Now you just need to be in the best mood to ignite your fireworks of ideas. Unfortunately, most of us are not necessarily euphoric at the sight of hundreds of spectators. Even groups of 10 members can cause sweating and stomach pain in some people. To make the situation easier for you, I have compiled a few tips on how to deal with this situation.

1. Count on the worst

I mean it just as I say it. Not everything will work. It won't work out exactly the way you imagined it. A speech will never be perfect. It's good if you make that clear to yourself beforehand. Then you don't have such a lot of quarreling with yourself afterwards.

Nervousness in this situation is something completely normal. It would be unnatural if you were not nervous. You might also get annoyed about that before.

2. Test your voice

If you've celebrated a roaring party the night before, you can't go on stage at 8 a.m. the next morning without them hearing that you drank beer or wine. The voice needs time to "sit" again after drinking alcohol and even after long periods of sleep. I don't drink alcohol at all at fairs where I have to talk all day. If I absolutely have to, I get up at least two hours earlier and talk myself in. I sing in the car, I look for a conversation partner for breakfast. Clearing my throat and coughing doesn't help. A conversation or a slight humming is much better.

3. Test the technique

I know I'm a little pedantic, but I don't go on stage without a detailed technical rehearsal, especially when I'm working with slides or films. An empty battery can lead to a disaster. I usually work with a headset or a clip-on microphone, but of course I have tested the hand microphone for emergencies. The hand microphone belongs in the inactive hand, so that as little kinetic energy as possible flows off. I already have the headset on my head 20 minutes ahead of time, so that I can determine whether it moves when I move.

4. Test the stage

I go up and down my stage first to see if there's back coupling somewhere or if the stage might crack. I also need to know where the light is and if it's blinding. It's usually no problem at all to turn or dim a spotlight. Most speakers just don't dare to talk about it. Sometimes I even make signs on the floor where I should walk. This can also be very helpful, for example, so that you don't stand in the projection screen of the beamer.

You can also adjust the height of lecterns. In addition, there are often a lot of things from past events lying around. I tidy it all up beforehand.

How often have I experienced that the flipchart of the predecessor could be seen very prominently during the entire presentation of the next speaker. You have to discuss and organize this beforehand.

5. Better too quiet than too loud

Of course, this only applies if you work with a microphone. A microphone is there to amplify your voice, and it doesn't make sense to roar into a microphone, apart from the moderation of a rock concert. Your voice gets a much more voluminous sound when you speak more quietly and you have to exert yourself less. And if you expect your voice to get louder by itself during the performance, tell the sound engineer beforehand.

6. For emergencies

I always have a handkerchief in my pocket. It has almost never been used, but I feel safer. What should I do if I have a slimy cough attack, sweat drops on my forehead or a saliva thread in the corner of my mouth? In addition, the glass with water is ready to hand, a stick with a copy of the presentation is near the stage, and a second felt-tip pen is next to it.

7. Tension and relaxation

Most people know what relaxes them and what doesn't. The thought of a warm summer day by the sea is often enough to calm me down a little. In addition, I turn off everything that could distract me. No relationship talks before the lecture, no e-mails and no strenuous small talk.

It may be advisable to skip the coffee on this day. The occasion offers enough excitement.

8. Eating and drinking

I plan a lecture from behind. When I perform at 4 p.m., lunch at 2 o'clock must not be the last thing I have eaten. After 2 p.m. I don't eat anything, especially heavy or fat food. And please don't eat anything sweet shortly before. After enjoying a chocolate bar, the mouth needs half an hour before it is ready for use. With a sticky mouth, a key note becomes really exhausting.

The same applies to toilet visits. These are also planned backwards.

9. Shortly before

In the last hour before the lecture, don't practice, don't edit, and don't count backwards. There are no fixed recommendations. I like to walk because it reduces my tension. But I don't discuss with the organizer how exciting everything is now. This makes everything even more exciting.

10. Have fun

I mean this literally: Imagine how much fun it will be for you and how much more fun it will be for you.

The end

A good speaker doesn't overdo it and doesn't use the opportunity to call as many people as possible at the end as many messages as possible in the ever decreasing time. Don't just come to the end when a third of the viewers are about to leave. Don't start pre-talking about internet addresses, pointing out books or downloading the data for the next gigs. They did that ten minutes ago, if it was absolutely necessary. Save yourself endings like

Well, I guess that's it, then.

I think I could answer most of the questions. Still questions?

I'm a little over the time. So let's make it short. Thanks for listening.

Don't apologize for things that went wrong during the lecture. Why warm it up again at the end? You should have done that long ago.

You also answered questions beforehand. Now you are coming to the end. And that is planned. Staged. It has a rhythm and there are a few clever thoughts in it, not just a summary of what we heard 20 minutes ago.

They become calmer. They become more specific. Now comes the last thought, the last story, the last sentence. The good speaker shows the way, gives tips on how to proceed.

And you can again use all the 100 possibilities I have shown you for the beginning:

From the thought of how much you felt honored, to the movie, from the magic trick to the changed quote. A few words of thanks, for example, would be very unusual here, so they would be better noticed and more effective than at the beginning.

Do not stop without a concluding sentence, a sentence whose sole purpose is to end the speech. The audience would otherwise feel surprised, thrown out, put out in front of the door. The final sentence is part of the speech.

However, I personally always make sure that in the end it becomes profound that the last message is something that can resonate, something that you might take home with you. Something that sticks and that occupies the audience on their way to their car or bus.

Then there's a broad and slow, important and simple, clear and flawless, crisp last sentence that you've well thought through.

Not too long, easy to keep and possibly funny. It must sit like the drumbeat at the end of a symphony. Depending on the theme loud and full of enthusiasm or quiet with fine irony. Ever slower with a pause before and after. After all, everyone should realize that now is the end. Otherwise the spectators don't know when to applaud.

The speaker looks at everyone very determinedly and safely stands firmly on both legs, is serenity itself. Possibly they smile with a winning smile. And if it was nice, if everyone has listened to him, if you've spent a stimulating hour together, then the speaker say at the final words: "Thank you!"

Like an actor, I bow at the end. I can't help it, because I deliver something like a paid performance for most speeches. I am booked and bow when I have delivered my performance.

But depending on the occasion, this seems inappropriate and bowing would be out of place. But if you want: Be courageous. That, too, is a form of appreciation. Maybe you just nod your head briefly and friendly as a sign that you are happy.

The professional ends exactly 30 seconds before or after the agreed time.

Mentioned books

Danz, Gerriet, Wilberg, Tim: An die Wand geworfen. Die lustigsten Powerpointpräsentationen von Angela Merkel bis zum Weihnachtsmann, München Wilhelm Heyne Verlag 2014

Jarvis, Jeff, What would google do? Reverse Engineering the Fastest-Growing Company in the History of the World, Collins, 2009

Nöllke, Matthias: Starke Worte – Einfach eine gute Rede halten. Wie Sie Ihre Zuhörer informieren, bewegen, überzeugen. München: Beck, 2015.

Rossié, Michael: Sprechertraining. Texte präsentieren in Radio, Fernsehen und vor Publikum. Wiesbaden: Springer VS, 2013, 5.Auflage

Skipwith, Thomas: Der Wurm muss dem Fisch schmecken - Mit Power präsentieren und rhetorisch punkten. Zürich: Orell Füssli, 2011

Tucholsky, Kurt, Ratschläge für einen schlechten Redner, in Gesammelte Werke, Rowohlt 1990

Watzlawick, Paul: The Situation is Hopeless, But Not Serious: The Pursuit of Unhappiness, Norton Company, 1993

Mentioned speaker and speeches

Page 28 /Page 49 Margit Hertlein (www.margit-hertlein.de)
Page 38 Francis Zentz (www.francisfromfrance.com)
Page 39 Markus Hofmann (www.unvergesslich.de)
Page 41 Denise Maurer (www.DeniseMaurer.de)
Page 45 Robert Spengler (www.robert-spengler.de)
Page 47 Frans Reichardt (www.fransreichardt.com)
Page 48 Ulrike Aichhorn (www.die-aichhorn.com)
Page 58/86 Thomas Skipwith (www.thomas-skipwith.com)
Page 59 Stefan Verra (www.stefanverra.com)
Page 67 Derek Arden (www.Derekarden.co.uk)
Page 68/69 Christine Weiner (www.christine-weiner.de)
Page 72 Daniel Gilbert "Why we make bad decisions"
(www.youtube.com)
Page 74 Thorsten Havener (thorsten-havener.com)
Page 79 Peter Zinn (www.peterzinn.nl)
Page 80 Lothar Seiwert (www.lothar-seiwert.de)
Page 80 Stefan Spies (www.profil360.com)
Page 85 Scott Stratten (www.unmarketing.com)
Page 85 Thomas Göller (www.goeller-mentoring.de)
Page 86 Don Yaeger (donyaeger.com)
Page 86 Nigel Risner (www.nigelrisner.com)
Page 86 Dave Newman (www.doitmarketing.com)
Page 87 Lore Lorentz (wikipedia.org/wiki/Lore_Lorentz)
Page 90 Gerhard Polt (poltseite.de)
Page 90 Slatco Sterzenbach (www.slatco-sterzenbach.com)
Page 92 Michael Ehlers (www.michael-ehlers.de)
Page 92 Gaston Florin (www.gaston-florin.de)
Page 92 Michael Sporer (www.michaelsporer.com)
Page 100 Klaus J. Fink (www.klaus-fink.de)
Page 100 Andreas Bornhäußer (www.praesentainment.de)
Page 103 Sally Hogshead (www.howtofascinate.com)
Page 104 Edgar K. Geffroy (www.geffroy.com)

Page 105 Gaby S. Graupner (www.gabysgraupner.de)
Page 106 John Bohannon, "Dance vs. PowerPoint, a modest proposal" (www.youtube.com)
Page 107 Colin Robertson, "A TED speaker's worst nightmare" (www.ted.com)

The author

Michael Rossié has been working as a language trainer and coach for radio and television stations, as well as in all areas of business for 30 years.

He attended the acting school Ruth v. Zerboni in Munich followed by theatre and film roles as well as engagements as director and trainer of actors and presenters. He also wrote screenplays for various television series.

In his seminars he shows new ways to communicate before and with groups. He has published 12 books so far.

Since 2012, Michael Rossié has been Vice President of the German Speakers' Association (GSA) and a member of the Top 100 of Speakers Excellence. Since 2013 he has been the twelfth German to bear the title CSP (Certified Speaking Professional).